S0-ABO-592

Hey, Lady! How Did You Get Way Up Here?

Climbing the 4000 Footers of New Hampshire

by
Judy Fracher

Durand Press   **Etna, NH**

About the Author

JUDY FRACHER was born in Portsmouth, New Hampshire in 1947. She married her childhood sweetheart, Mike, with whom she raised two children. Today, they have three grandchildren. Judy has worked in the Portsmouth Regional Hospital in various capacities since she was eleven years old and currently works as a nurse in the Short Stay Unit and the Recovery Room. A lifetime Girl Scout, she has held many posts - most recently as First Aid Trainer. Judy enjoys almost any activity. Her favorites include hiking, square and round dancing, playing Parcheesi, swimming, cross country skiing and romantic windjammer cruises. An avid reader, she usually has at least two books to read simultaneously and reads everything from cereal boxes to Tolstoy. Judy attends seminars on subjects of Psychic Development, reads Tarot Cards, and does Palmistry for fun. She gains much from personal meditation. Her philosophy of life is a simple one—you do not have to be particularly good at an activity to enjoy it.

Illustrator: Trevor Bartlett
Editor: Carol Grosky
Front cover photo: Mount Carragain from Zealand Notch, courtesy of The Durand Press; back cover photo courtesy of the author
© 1996 Judy Fracher All rights reserved.

Published by the Durand Press
374 Dogford Road
Etna, NH 03750-4310

ISBN Number   0-9633560-4-6

Printed in the United States of America by BookCrafters.
Typesetting and design by Nomad Communications, Norwich, VT.
The text of this book is set in Minion by Adobe.

Imprint is the last number shown: 9 8 7 6 5 4 3 2 1

TABLE OF CONTENTS

ACKNOWLEDGMENTS

THIS BOOK could never have been written without the help, support, and encouragement of my husband, Michael. He did not complain about being a bachelor/baby sitter when I took to the hills. He joined me on a great many climbs and encouraged me to accomplish my goals. He was particularly helpful during hypothermia episodes on camping trips. One might say that he saved my hide on more than one occasion.

My two children, Michael and Kristyn, shared several summits with me and it was a thrill to follow behind them (way behind them) as they literally left me in a cloud of dust—only to await my arrival at the top. I hope to have infected them with the hiking bug which, even if it lies dormant in them for decades, may bite them later in life. With luck, this bug will someday bite my grandchildren. I thank them for the wonderful memories they gave me.

I also owe a huge thank you to Nancy and Carl Seavey and Carla Marvin without whom I probably could not have finished the four thousand footers. Also thanks to Carol Pearson and Carol Adams, Ed Yeganeh, Joe and Rachel Wallace, Mary Gaudreau, Gaylene Chaloult, Art Batchelder, and Jim, Tracy and Sean Wilton for their company and for joining forces to push me along to achieve my goal. Hugs also to my ground-bound friend, Evelyn Wyatt, who could not understand the drive to achieve my goal, but encouraged me anyway.

Finally a prayer for the late George Patten who advised me for several years on all the aspects of hiking and camping and now joins me in Spirit whenever I put on a backpack.

Thanks and love to all of you. I really could not have done it without you!

INTRODUCTION

THE MOST common questions are why and how. Why someone my age, weight, and physical condition would climb the four thousand footers of New Hampshire, and how someone my age, weight, and physical condition *could* climb these mountains. It took me almost the whole 48 climbs, a few accidents, and much introspective thought to get my own answers to those two questions.   I climbed my first two mountains when I was in the Girl Scouts in 1963. Bill Feaster, a local minister's son, guided our troop up Sugarloaf and then Katahdin. I remember my best friend, Tessie Follansbee, and I skidding across

Knife Edge on our buttocks because we were too scared to stand upright. I came down the rest of the trail with the proverbial bare behind! I wore out the seat of my jeans! I remember getting to the top and enjoying a great feeling of accomplishment which was replaced by lameness the following morning. If memory serves, I could not manage stairs for several days. I was glad to have gone on the trip-and proud to have attained the summit, but I viewed it as a once in a lifetime event. I had no urge to repeat the experience.

In 1980, I experienced a few episodes of moderately severe chest pain. Considering my family history, I had a medical work-up which eventually led me to Boston and the Massachusetts General Hospital. After a series of stress exercise tests I was given a very disturbing diagnosis: obesity, an untrained state, and out of condition. I may be, shall we say, big-boned, and untrained, but out of shape—wrong! At the time, I was playing competitive racquetball and was, at least in my own opinion, very active. The diagnosis cut me to the core. The words sort of sat there in the back of my mind... annoying me. That summer, while we were relaxing at our retreat, I packed up my unsuspecting kinfolk and off we went to climb Mount Washington. We chose to take the Ammonoosuc Ravine Trail and off we went. It was a great family adventure. Just below the peak, I found my second wind. We made it... all of us. I took a rather tacky photo at the top by the Mount Washington Observatory and mailed it to my doctor in Boston. When we returned to the cottage I swam the mile across the lake. That night I went to sleep much more contented with myself. Incidentally, the aforementioned photo was sent back to my local physician, who accidentally drops it out of my folder every time I go to the office.

So why do I climb? I admit that I get short of breath putting on my boots. I admit that within ten minutes or less on the trail, I think I am making a big mistake. I do not remember why I am doing this to myself. I am old enough to do what I want when I want, but here I am hauling butt up some mountain. Then I get to the top and the same words come to mind every time. I look around, pull off my pack, take a really deep breath, and think, "This is why I do this..." The colors of the mountains—the lush greens of early spring, the verdant shades of summer and the shocking colors of the fall—none of those are quite the same from the roadways. I stand there feeling that I have conquered the world, and that that world is me. I love the mountains and enjoy taking people up to their first peak. I see what I am feeling reflected in their faces. I feel at home and at peace with myself and with God.   If you look at the bottom of some of the AMC maps, you will see the name R.Lennox. He and his friends revised and edited some of the AMC's maps of the White Mountains. Some of the maps were done on his kitchen table. I was privileged to be able to read Bob's journal. In it was an explanation of his feelings about hiking. I think this says it for most of us.

"I wish it were possible to find the words to express the feelings we had as we stood on the summit of fabled Chocorua's great cone of granite and observed the beauty and grandeur of the mountains and its view. If I could convey the feelings of serenity and peacefulness, of accomplishment, and well-being, then you might know why we climb mountains."

Judy Fracher
Portsmouth, NH

MOUNT WASHINGTON

Elevation: 6288
Date: July 18, 1980
Trail: Ammonoosuc Ravine

I COULD not believe that I actually got up so early… me, the one who always worked the afternoon shift so I could sleep late in the day. Yet, there I was, up and breakfasted by seven in the morning and on vacation no less! Mike and I were very enthusiastic about this adventure and we managed to transfer our feelings to our two children. It was to be a classic family outing. I found my old Girl Scout pack in the attic. It was a faded green canvas bag that needed much adjustment since the last time it had been on a body was seventeen years earlier.

Thoughts of the Mount Katahdin climb rolled through my mind causing twin twinges of remembered pain in my calves. I chose to keep those negative thoughts to myself.

We piled into our car and began the trip up Route 16. We sang a few songs, played a few license plate identification games and other road games to keep up the camaraderie in the family until, in the distance, appeared the peak of Mount Washington. It was a clear day and the smoke from the Cog Railway billowed blackly against the white cloud-studded summer sky. Assailed by a vague feeling of fear, I pasted a smile on my face and kept up a constant flow of inane chatter. Michael, our oldest at age eleven, looked up and gave me a look that assured me that one thing was certain—we would pay dearly if this trip turned out as he was suspecting it would. Kristyn, our youngest, aged nine, looked up and seemed confused... she was still innocent enough to believe that her parents would not ask her to do anything as dangerous, as stupid, or as impossible as attaining that peak.

We inquired at the railway station for the safest trail to use to make our ascent, and were told to take the Ammonoosuc Ravine Trail both up and down. We found the trail blazes as directed and stepped into the cool woods. It was nice to enter the forest because from there, it was no longer possible to see the top of the mountain. We gave the children free-rein and they set a very good pace, stopping often to look at the mushrooms, flowers, bugs, and ferns. We were all enjoying the day.

The stream, the Ammonoosuc River, was a lovely one and most of the trail went along side of it, or over it. It had a picture perfect quality and it was difficult to prevent the children- or ourselves-from dipping our hands into the stream for a cold drink. At one point, after crossing a foot bridge, we came upon a waterfall that cascaded down into an emerald-colored pool.

It was a magical spot that would have taken my breath away if I had had any breath left in me at the time. We took a nice break by this spot and watched the sun dapple the vegetation and make the stones in the pool appear to be gold. Not a sound disturbed the quiet.

All too soon, we began the ascent along the falls. The way became steeper and steeper with each step. Oftentimes we needed to help each other over the huge boulders. Everyone's face was reddened by the exertion, and our breathing was ragged, but no one wanted to give up. We had a non-verbal pact between us now. We would make it—all of us.

We came suddenly upon a clearing and much to our surprise, a large wooden building was there. People with packs were walking in and out of it. We were concerned that this might be private property and that the owners might make us backtrack and we would have to climb up a different way. We quietly walked by. We were later to learn that we would have been welcomed at the building, for it was the Appalachian Mountain Club's Lake of the Clouds Hut. Mountain hospitality at its best. Sitting by one of the small lakes and cooling our tired feet was perfect. Our lunch consisted of heavenly peanut butter sandwiches, peaches, Kool-Aid and candy bars. Food never tasted so good.

We all seemed to get a second wind after lunch and the children took off like mountain goats—bouncing from boulder to boulder. The balance of the hike to the top was mostly over brown lichen-covered rocks with odd fragile flowers in between them. After seeing a flower shatter like frozen glass, we left them alone.

We arrived at the summit in a seemingly short time compared to the rest of the hike. We toured through the building until we had to go back down. We were all impressed by the stories of the people who winter all alone up on the mountain and were fascinated by the photographs of the frozen wasteland which exists there so many months of the year. Our trip down the mountain was much faster than the ascent. We were all filled with the wonder of what we had accomplished and enjoyed a feeling of family togetherness. It had been a great trip.

Hey, Lady!

CARTER–WILDCAT

CARTER DOME Elevation: 4832
WILD CAT Elevation: 4422
WILD CAT E Elevation: 4041
Dates: July 27-28, 1984
Trails: Nineteen Mile Brook Trail
Wildcat Ridge Trail

MARY GAUDREAU and I decided to get a little exercise and to celebrate my thirty-seventh birthday out in the woods. After a short deliberation, we chose to do Carter Dome and the Wildcats. The reason for this selection escapes me, but it was probably due to the proximity to the highway and the fact that it seemed pretty straight forward in the *AMC Guidebook*—an early gift. We decided to add a bit of flair and style to the woods and took a couple of days to coordinate our outfits. Mary chose an ensemble of tans and reds and I chose lavenders and grays.

We were matching from our bandanna heads to our hiking boots and backpacks. Yes, we were a vision!

Mike dropped us off at the trailhead for the Nineteen-Mile Brook Trail—ominous name, that. We hoped the name was not literal, but were sure that in our coordinated outfits, we would conquer all. We turned away to enter the woods. Mike drove off. The skies opened. After a very few minutes, Mary and I resembled drowned Druids. The rest of the day, we plodded along in and out of torrential rains. So much for the visions!

We took many breaks along the way—to examine with breathless wonder the number of colors of mushrooms on and off the trail, the stream, the sky, the flowers… actually, any excuse to stop and lean over to breathe was welcome. At lunch time, there was an attempt made to erect a lean-to under which we would ideally stay dry long enough to eat lunch. The attempt failed miserably when one corner of the structure emptied upon Mary's shoulder. We managed to plod on. I had to wonder if just looking at some mushrooms too closely could cause hallucinations, as both Mary and I found ourselves seeing things that were not there in the woods… like large animals and once, a tree hut. We started to hesitate to point out the sights to each other!

Rather high up on the trail appeared a pile of wood with a sign that asked passersby to carry some wood up to the hut. Renewed, because we saw this as a sure sign that we were near our goal, we graciously grabbed a few pieces of wood and actually managed to move them several feet up the trail before having to give up and put them back down. We soon reached an area that thankfully went downhill. We slowly picked our way down the trail and found ourselves in the middle of a Stephen Speilberg Jurassic Park movie set. On either side of the trail were twenty-five foot (or more) monoliths rising out of primordial waters. The rain had stopped for a time and the ground was covered in an eerie blanket of swirling ankle high mist. The trail continued for what seemed like a half an hour before we reached a large lake. The appearance of a Loch Ness monster or a huge reptilian bird swooping down from the cliffs above would have come as absolutely no surprise to us. Dodging real and imaginary creatures, we joined a group of French students in the attempt to climb to the summit of Carter Dome. The trail to the top was particularly difficult with large boulders. It seemed very steep and dangerous. We arrived at the summit in a complete blanket of fog. I could not even see my shoes, let alone any scenery. We cautiously picked our way back down to the hut.

The Carter Notch Hut is actually made up of several buildings spread out on the side of the mountain. We did not notice how many because we never could see more than a foot or two in front of our faces. After checking in at the main building, we ascended stone stairs and arrived at our bunk house. On the porch were two gentlemen drying their socks. Obviously a mistake had been made. We hauled ourselves back down the hill only to find to our eternal amazement that these two men were our roommates for the night. Co-ed! We were not at all sure how to handle this situation. I was concerned that I had not read the AMC Guide correctly as to procedures and behavior, while Mary kept laughing about what her husband, Ron, would make of this. We decided to be very blase about the whole thing and again hauled ourselves up over the hill. We nicknamed our roomies Prince Charles and Philip. They chivalrously left the area while Mary and I prepared for supper. They offered us sardines and marshmallows, a combination I had never, nor will ever try!

Supper was a great memory. Mary had mentioned to the

Hutmaster that it was my birthday. We had a home-cooked meal of ham, salads, fresh-baked breads, soups and vegetables. For dessert, I was presented with a piece of peach cobbler with a hurricane candle sticking out of it. The whole room sang Happy Birthday to me and, surprisingly, it did not embarrass me at all. I liked it!

Mary and I stayed overlong at the main building, probably to avoid facing our roommates. It was now the blackest, darkest night I had ever seen in my life and unfortunately, we had left our flashlights in our bunk room. We literally crawled up the hillside, feeling along the steps with our hands. Mary was fixated on being eaten by a bear while I, being more practical, worried about falling off the edge of the world and being attacked by Dinosaurs. In a light rain Mary and I made it to the bath house where Mary chose to change into her night wear. I chose to stay dry and change in the darkness of our room. After all, I could not see my own hand in front of my face, so surely Philip and Charles would be equally blessed. I had not counted on my friend Mary. I carefully laid out my Barbizon nightie… just so. Then in total darkness and absolute silence, I undressed. I could not find the hole in the gown and muttered a harmless expletive. My friend turned her thousand-watt flashlight dead on me. I was surprised and blinded! I stood there frozen like a deer caught in the headlights of a car. I hope the rest of the room was equally blinded… but I think, just think, I remember a chuckle or two from the upper bunks before the darkness swallowed me up again.

We were awakened by the Hut Crew to a full and perfect breakfast. I only wished that my stomach had awakened as early as I had. I took several bites of everything and saved the fruit for the next part of the hike. Mary was in rare form that day. We climbed to the top of the hill where the trail forks. We could

either go down the Nineteen-mile Brook Trail, or forge ahead to the Wildcats. Mary had, I should mention, injured her leg imitating the Flying Walendas the previous day during an attempt to cross a foot bridge. She was wearing my grandfather's Navy scarf tied tightly around her thigh. She voted to go onward and upward. Most of the day was a blur because we were in fog from way above our heads to just below our knees. At one point, we saw a sign that said OUTLOOK and we went to see what that meant. We were soon atop a cliff overlooking... nothing. It was as if the world had turned into a sea of milk. I had the feeling that if I stepped off the cliff, I would be able to stand on the clouds, for they looked quite solid. It was amazing. The Wildcat Range was not quite as it was portrayed on the maps. On the map appear about five humps, whereas in reality it has at least twenty. Since we could not see any signs anywhere, I feared the first road we came to might well be in Georgia. It was a relief to hear the Wildcat Gondola as it gave us some idea of where we were. By then, Mary and I had deteriorated. She was threatening me with a tiny Swiss Knife to stop the hike and I was bribing her with Gummybears to keep moving. We were a sorry sight! We continued on.

After getting down the mountain, we avoided being hit by the traffic on Route 16 and checked into the AMC's nearby Pinkham Notch Base Camp. By then, Mary was in substantial pain from her injury, and I ached just about everywhere. One of the finest things about Pinkham is that it has warm rooms and showers. Fortunately, a man and his son took pity on us and helped us through the evening meal by fetching us food and drinks. We were treated to a Chamber Quartet and Kahlua—straight—on the porch after supper. When we returned to our room, Mary presented me with a great birthday gift... a bottle of wine that she had hauled up all those moun-

Hey, Lady!

tains. What a friend! We unskillfully opened the cork and it made a huge bang. The people in the next room came running with Crew Members. Apparently they thought the sound was a rifle and they came looking for bodies! We shared a laugh and the wine with them.

After breakfast, we lounged about wishing we had the energy to climb to the Cascades. We read, visited, and watched others take off for more hiking. Our husbands came to pick us up mid-afternoon and took us to a restaurant in Meredith, New Hampshire for supper. During the drive to the restaurant, we sat still, relating our adventures to our spouses. By the time we arrived at our destination, our muscles had tightened up. We managed to hobble in for a dinner which was a brilliant end to the perfect weekend.

SOUTHERN PEAKS

MOUNT JACKSON Elevation: 4052
MOUNT EISENHOWER Elevation: 4761
MOUNT PIERCE Elevation: 4310
Date: September 1-2, 1984
Trails: Webster Cliff, Crawford Path
Edmand's Path

TWO MONTHS had passed since the conquering of Carter Dome and the Wildcats and I felt the need to go up to the hills once more. Mary was not quite ready to toss her hat back into the climbers' circle. After some heavy-duty whining, Mike agreed to accompany me on my next adventure. At this point in time, my goal was not to finish the four-thousand footers, but to get out and do something different. We picked the mountains, and I picked the trails after careful deliberation and map study. It was the beginning of a skill that many have come to

Hey, Lady!

respect. I can usually find the shortest and easiest way up any mountain! We decided to spend one night at the Mizpah Spring Hut before hiking back to the highway the next day. I felt better about having Mike along to stay with me at the hut.

Mike and I got up early and I unsuccessfully tried to stuff French toast down a still-asleep stomach. The children were staying over at friends' homes, so we only needed to deal with two small neurotic dogs skulking about looking very concerned about their parents being up and about before first light. They would not be consoled. I managed to fight sleep as we drove north. The scenery flew by in a panorama of color—the rises and falls of colorful mountain tops and valleys. It was a visual lullaby and my eyes closed and my head nodded forward as Mike drove. We arrived at the Willey House Station where we were to leave our car for the hike. In the parking lot, we divvied up the packs and possessions and crossed the highway to begin the climb up the Webster Cliff Trail. We started out at a pace much faster than the one Mary and I had set the last time, but the terrain was not too steep at first and it was not difficult to maintain the speed. Mike had a theory about fluid consumption that he had learned in high school and in the Army. It consisted of merely sip, swish, and spit out... no swallowing. I bowed to his superior knowledge of physiology and exercise and gave it a try. I proceeded to dehydrate slowly. A short time before we arrived at Webster Overlook, I got hit with a slight case of the runs. This helped the dehydration process along nicely, and before too long Mike stopped me from my ascent. My face had changed from a stressed red to a burning maroon. It was quickly determined that I did not fit the class of either football player or soldier, and I was given permission to drink and wear a sporty red bandanna soaked in cool water. As we stood talking, I realized that we were standing rather unbalanced at a 45 degree angle. Somehow I had missed the trail becoming more steep and had been trying to maintain the speed we had started with. We slowed down.

Arriving at the Overlook, we stood in awe as we looked down at the purple ribbon of highway below us. The sun was shining brightly at the time and the warmth of the day and beauty of the surroundings were a gentle balm on our spirits. We reluctantly left the cliff and forged onward. The Webster Cliff Trail is well-marked and easy to follow. A series of switchbacks to the summit makes the trail longer than a direct route would be, but it is less stressful to the ecology and for the hiker.

We arrived at the top of Mount Jackson just about time for lunch. I was starved and very thirsty by then. There was not a soul around and we found a sheltered area to sit and rest. Mike took off his shirt and spread it on a scrub brush to dry. After assuring myself that we were out of the sight of anything but a plane flying sideways, I removed my wet shirt too. There was a slightly cool breeze and in my innocence and ignorance, I thought it better to dry my shirt rather than to avoid the chilly breeze. We lunched on deviled ham sandwiches, cookies and fruit. The scenery from this elevation was fantastic, almost making up for what Mary and I had missed from the other peaks. As I watched with amazement, a dark cloud approached and enveloped us in rain. It happened in less than a minute. Sunshine to shower. We quickly donned our re-wet clothes and scampered down the trail. I became cold very quickly. Mike said that we had to hurry to reach the hut and set a rather unfair pace. As I walked along behind, my mind started to go fuzzy. Everything was funny... from watching Mike go further and further ahead, to the fact that I kept falling off my hiking boots. I rarely chuckled to myself back then, but I was certainly amused that day. Finally the fact that something might

Hey, Lady!

actually be wrong with me penetrated my fog and when I caught up with the pace setter, he figured out what that something could be. He had had the sense to don a wool shirt and he quickly put it on me. I changed my mind somewhat about wool that day. Instead of vowing to never wear that itchy fiber, I would definitely carry it from now on for near death experiences. Looking back, I assume that I had a sort of hypothermia incident and I have discovered that it does not take a very long time for some people (like myself) to fall victim to this potentially dangerous condition.

Fortunately, the sun chose that moment to reappear and we were only a few yards from our goal—the Mizpah Spring Hut. A cup of hot soup and a hot cocoa restored me. We joined others at the hut in spreading out our wet clothes on the lawn to dry. We were later encouraged to finish the drying process in a warming closet reminiscent of the ones in London. There is an attic space located directly above the kitchen area and the heat from the kitchen keeps the attic dry and warm enough to encourage clothes drying. Mizpah, built in 1965, consists of one building. The crew was all young and super-efficient. All were made welcome and we enjoyed a filling meal and a very amusing evening's entertainment provided by crew and guests alike. We decided that we would return someday to go to the quaking bog, but did not feel up to it that day. The bog is a swampy area that moves in unpredictable ways when a person walks on it. The crew did not fully explain the bog to us, as they wanted to encourage us to experience it for ourselves. We slept like babies that night.

The next day, a fog bank rolled in during breakfast. The Crew announced that visibility was almost nil and that we should be careful hiking. After my experience the day before, I dressed warmly. We donned our rain gear because of the fog.

It was not raining per se, but the whole area was soaked and we would have been wet within minutes. I soon discovered that a person with glasses has a decided disadvantage in fog and rain. I was blind. Mike wore a white tee-shirt on his backside to give me something I could spot. We slowed our speed considerably. Fortunately the trail was easy to stay on and not as difficult as the one we had done the day before. We talked a lot, and did not bother to take breaks at first and were very surprised to see a sign confirm that we had arrived at the top of Mount Pierce, alias Mount Clinton. Since there were no views, we ate the fruit from breakfast and were soon on our way along the Crawford Path to Mount Eisenhower. The trail became a bit more difficult and mucky at times, but all in all it was a pleasant hike. Our only regret was that Mother Nature seemed pretty determined to keep us from seeing the majesty that we knew was all around us. We found the Edmand's Path and followed it out to the Mount Clinton Road. I think the worst part of the hike was at this point. We had to walk along the road until we reached the Crawford Depot. I was too tired to take another step and the car was much further down the highway. Mike volunteered to go on alone to get the car, promising to return for me. My Hero! He only walked about fifteen paces before a fellow hiker offered him a ride. Until Mike returned I lay by the side of the road like a well-seasoned hiker, probably looking and smelling like one also.

Hey, Lady!

MOUNT TECUMSEH

Elevation: 4004
Date: October 21, 1984
Trail: Mount Tecumseh Trail

FOUR YEARS had passed since we had climbed as a family. Our children were now teenagers. Michael, fifteen, was taller than me and Kristyn was now thirteen. Romance was in the air that gorgeous Fall morning. Kristyn's feeling of friendship for her brother's best friend, Enoch Kennett, had turned a tad more serious. Fortunately, Michael seemed pleased with the situation, and the three of them were all friendly and content with each other. Michael's birthday was in two days time and he had asked the right person to take him on a trip to the mountains… his mother! My husband, Mike, got caught up in the planning and soon our little group was set to go. Enoch spent the night so we could get an early start.

The car ride to the mountains was fantastic with much laughter and friendly talk. Michael and Enoch planned out all the war games they would be able to play on the ascent. Kristyn was content to listen and to sit between her brother and her beau. We were enjoying ourselves and each others' company. Even getting lost on the highway did not dampen our enthusiasm. We soon found our way to the base of the trail. We set some ground rules with the teenagers about potential dangers and about wandering off the trail and they set off—leaving us to follow at a much more leisurely pace.

The map shows two brooks on the trail, but I only remember the one to the right of the trail. It was a beautiful sight as we dodged in and out of the woods. The kids went further ahead and Mike and I, catching the romantic atmosphere, stopped at intervals for quick hugs and kisses. From the distance, we could hear the shouts of the boys intermingled with shrieks from Kristyn. Happiness abounded. Alas, the happiness would soon be tainted because the trail became steeper as we went along. Before too long, I felt like I was trying to suck my big toes up through my lungs with every breath. I told Mike to go on ahead to catch up with the children and that I would soon catch my breath and get to the summit on my own.

The summit was a bit of a disappointment with a few closed ski area buildings in the dead grass with none of them selling the hot coffee that my body craved. We broke for lunch and were amazed to see that it was beginning to spit snow. Unbelievable! We stood around catching the white crystals on the ends of our tongues for a time before we realized that we were not prepared for a Winter hike. We began a quick, graceless descent down the ski trail.

Hey, Lady!

**NORTH KINSMAN
MOUNTAIN**

Elevation: 4293
Date: June 29, 1985
Trails: Lonesome Lake Trail
Fishin' Jimmy Trail

MIKE AND I decided that it would be a wonderful way to sa-
lute Spring… to join the black flies, mosquitoes, and other creatures of the woods. We elected to go to Lonesome Lake Hut
and from there to ascend to North and South Kinsman. Our
offspring quickly found excuses not to join us and opted to
visit their grandmother. We made one of our now infamous
early starts and arrived at the Lafayette Place Campground in
time to see the campers waking up and to smell the wonderful
aroma of sizzling bacon and coffee brewing on open fires. Even

my sleeping stomach responded to the stimulation. We took a quick snack break at the start of the trail. It was easy to find the beginning of this trail, and the whole walk up was accented by many trail signs that assured me that we were on the right path.

All trails that are maintained by the AMC and other organizations such as the Dartmouth Outing Club, and the Boy Scouts have various ways to keep hikers going in the right direction. The majority use a combination of blazes, or paint marks placed at intervals on trees or rocks, with wooden signs with mileage and locations printed on them.

We arrived at Lonesome Lake in what seemed record time. We even had time to take a few photos by the lake before skirting around it to arrive and check in at the Lonesome Lake Hut. Before continuing to the summit we divided our possessions and packs and decided to take only one pack that we would take half-hourly turns carrying. What a great difference that made to me! I felt forty pounds lighter and bounded off ahead of my husband for the first time I could remember. We had chosen the Fishin' Jimmy Trail, more for the name than anything else, and except for a few muddy spots, we found that it was a relatively nice hike. Mike became quieter and quieter as we progressed.

We took quite a while to reach the top of North Kinsman and by then Mike admitted that he did not feel too well. He and I sat quietly side by side on the rocks enjoying the view of the giant Cannon Mountain and the Cannonballs off in the distance. He suggested that since South Kinsman was not too far away, I should take the pack and go to the next peak by myself. I made a decision that was to haunt me until 1991. I did not feel secure enough in my ability to go on alone. I decided to omit South Kinsman from my plan and just enjoy the day with Mike. In later years, when I decided to finish climbing the Four Thousand Footers, I would have to repeat this climb of North Kinsman because it stands between the highway and South Kinsman.

Since we had time to kill, we just stayed there to rest... not even talking. I never felt closer to Mike. I took a photo of him sitting on the edge of the mountain looking back at me and now I keep the picture in a silver frame. I never walk by it without stopping to look at it and remember the day with fondness.

We arrived back at the hut in the early afternoon and I decided that since the lake was so handy, I should take a dip. I could not for the life of me figure out why no one was in the water. The sun was high in the blue sky and even though it was only June, it was unseasonably hot. I changed into the suit that had somehow found its way into my pack, and down to the lake I went. The chill that shot through my body as I touched my toe to the water should have screamed a warning, but for some reason, it did not register. I bounded in with a shallow body dive. It was freezing! Pride was the only thing-other than the fact that my heart and lungs had suddenly ceased to function-that kept me from running out as fast as I had run in. After a few minutes, however, it was easier to tolerate. I paddled around until someone mentioned blood suckers and I decided that it was time to change for supper.

Lonesome Lake Hut is one of the most accessible AMC Huts. It is a favorite with families because of the easy ascent and the area around it. It has a main room with a common area and two bunkhouses. We were fortunate to have a guest speaker at the hut that night. He took us on a walk around the lake and told about the history of the area and about all the animals, including the beavers that come to enjoy the birch trees. He was a dynamic speaker and we clung to each pearl of wisdom he shared long into the evening.

This man was a prime example of the speakers and lecturers that the AMC sponsors. Throughout the year, talks are held both at the AMC's Boston Headquarters and in Pinkham Notch, and in the summer at the different huts on subjects covering many topics. It was a perfect day.

During the night, we were awakened by a commotion in the common area. Concerned, we dressed and went down to the main building where we found four older teens (dressed only in shorts and tee-shirts) being warmed by the Crew. It seemed these youngsters had started out late on a trail, had had a little too much beer, and had become lost. They were fortunate to find the hut. They would have spent a very cold uncomfortable night if they had not. The Crew did an admirable job in their chastisement, and put them to bed in the bunk house. In the morning, they led them to the trailhead leading down. We had a leisurely breakfast and listened to others plan their hikes for the day. We vicariously lived their days by listening to them. We started down the trail and arrived all too soon at the campground. The drive home was wonderful, and in very high spirits we began to plan future hikes.

Hey, Lady!

MOUNT HALE

Elevation: 4054
Date: October 12, 1985
Trails: Hale Brook Trail
Lend-a-Hand Trail
Zealand Trail

AT LAST Mary had had enough time to forget the pain and was ready to join me in another trek into the wilderness. Again we met to discuss and plan, not the trail, but our fashion. Our husbands just shrugged it off, but we really got into it! This time Mary was gorgeous in pinks, and I was a thing to behold in greens. We drove up to park on the paved road by Zealand Campground off the highway. We were bubbling with adolescent enthusiasm as we affixed our packs and hit the trail. We were soon surprised to see frozen ground that proved to be just a tad slippery. We denied to each other that it could possibly be snow. We strove to prevent ourselves from dirtying our new boots and the going was pretty slow for a while. The closer we got to the top, the more frozen ground we ran into and it was not too long before the denial was acknowledged… it was snow! The trail became a blur-putting one foot in front of the other and pushing and pulling ourselves up the slope. Fortunately every time we decided to just forget our climb, the trail became easier and we would forge on ahead. At the top of the mountain, we were surprised to see at least twenty people milling about. All of them were dressed in Winter gear and were discussing mountains and trails to take. Mary and I donned warmer clothes and sat nearby listening intently to all the exchanges. We ate our lunch, fascinated by those around us, and we watched them separate and silently slip onto different paths into the woods. All was quiet.

It became more chilly and we decided to head on to the Zealand Notch Hut… unfortunately we were not sure which path to take to get there. There were no signs telling us where to go. I realized that I could not remember which way we had come up either. Mary did not know how heavily the cloak of responsibility was lying on my shoulders. I had recently taken an orientation course and took out my trusty new compass and placed the map and the compass down. No dice. The rocks atop Mount Hale are magnetic and distort the compass readings. I was not experienced enough to make the corrections. Figuring that we could either freeze on Mount Hale, or end up on the road instead of at the hut, we picked a likely trail and cast our fates to the wind. We were concerned because we heard no noises of other hikers, nor did we see one of the precious blazes I had come to love and depend on. The pace became a little frenetic as we moved ever downward. Mary interjected humor into all this

Hey, Lady!

mess by writing our obituaries. Things like "When last seen, Judy was wearing an adorable green outfit with matching scarf and socks, while Mary was in a new creation by EMS in a stunning pink." She had me in tears as she pointed out that we had gone downhill in more ways than one. At the beginning of the trail, we had been so cautious about our appearance, and now here we were—filthy boots, socks uneven, and dirty, mud-stained legs barely keeping us on the trail.

Fortunately, the gods smiled upon us and we saw signs of civilization—mainly a few juice cartons. We also saw some huge rubber hoses going along the trail. We followed them and found the Zealand Falls Hut. We were warmly welcomed and the terror of the afternoon was quickly lost in the camaraderie of the group. The sun felt hot on our backs, and there was no evidence of the snow we had seen that morning. We sat out on the rocks in the stream by the Falls and it seemed that time stood still and we were able to actually watch the leaves turn color. We enjoyed a wonderfully prepared supper of chicken, vegetable stir-fry and wild rice and went to sleep like tired babies.

Breakfast was a fun and noisy affair. The only problem I could see was that all the water, even the juice, tasted of Iodine. Mary and I joined several other hikers just above the Hut enjoying a taste of the fresh running water of Zealand Falls. It began to rain lightly as we began our descent. The trail down started out quite steep and then leveled out and Mary and I could walk side by side and actually walk and talk at the same time. However, we had a lesson to learn from the mountain. The lesson is a simple one: "IF THE WATER AT A HUT TASTES OF IODINE, DO NOT DRINK FROM THE STREAM!"

Iodine, or sometimes bleach, is used to purify water that may not be safe to drink due to bacteria. Even the slight case of Montezuma's Revenge did not dampen our spirits as we walked along a wonderful trail stopping only to dig little cat trenches. Nancy Seavey, a friend from work and an excellent hiker, had told me to leave a complete change of clothes and a towel in the car when I hiked, so Mary and I were able to get completely dry and went home, slightly crampy, but wiser.

When I arrived home, I found that Mike had prepared a wonderful meal from his new Frugal Gourmet Cookbook. It was fantastic and afterwards I relaxed in our Jacuzzi. It was the perfect end to a not-quite-so-perfect day.

FRANCONIA RIDGE

MOUNT LINCOLN   Elevation: 5089
MOUNT LAFAYETTE   Elevation: 5260
Date: September 17, 1987
Trail: Falling Waters Trail
        Franconia Ridge Trail
        Greenleaf Trail

NO HIKING since October 1985! It had been a terrible two years for me as I had been laid up with a disc problem caused by doing a flying half-gainer out the back door while letting the dog out. Who ever expected ice that early in the season? For too long my days consisted of working part-time at the hospital as a nurse and then hobbling about trying to keep the home and family functioning normally. Climbing was out of the question. Finally, after spring and summer 1987 had passed me by, I decided that enough was enough. If I could not get better physically, I might as well do something about my mental health. Carla Marvin, a fellow nurse, agreed to accompany me on a hike to Mount Lafayette and Mount Lincoln. We would stay at the Greenleaf Hut. We agreed that if we could not make it all the way, we would turn back with no regrets. Carla and I did not coordinate outfits. We dressed for comfort. We were both in shorts, but we carried warmer clothes in our packs. Sleep was almost impossible the night before the climb. I was so excited about getting back up in the mountains again. Mike was crazy from my tossing and turning all night long. It was like Christmas Eve for a child! I was up and about at four-thirty in the morning with no way to control my nervous energy. In the quiet of the still-asleep household, I dressed and then slipped into the kitchen to put on my hiking boots. All my feelings were so intense. I was excited about hiking again, fearful of failing, worried about getting hurt, and anxious to get going. I could not seem to expand any particular thought long enough to explore how I felt. Carla called to see if we could go earlier than planned. I was biting my car keys by then, so off we went. We stopped by Jeanine's Bakery in Portsmouth for breakfast.

The drive up Franconia Notch was beautiful; the vibrant Fall colors were made all the brighter by an uplifted spirit. Carla and I talked comfortably and got to know each other much better than we had by working together. We parked in the Lafayette Campground parking area right off the main highway and soon found our way to the start of the trail. It was not long before I began to wonder why I had not stayed on the couch while I had the chance. The going was pretty rough, my pack shifted awkwardly on my back, and I was certainly out of shape. Carla was a beginner at hiking that day but it was the first and the last time I was to ever be ahead of her on a trail.

Hey, Lady!

She would join on AMC sponsored hikes later that year and become an excellent hiker. I am pleased to have been with her on her first hike! We were wheezing and rasping, and our conversation reduced to mere grunts when we came upon a fantastic sight. In the distance off to our right appeared a huge mirror. It looked to be about 100 feet long and was quite wide. With the morning sun reflecting off it, it seemed to be made of glass. Later we learned that this is a giant rock slide with water cascading down the face. Once in a while the sun hits it just right to cause the mirror effect that we had seen.

We arrived at the summit of Little Haystack shortly thereafter, and from then on, there was not an ache or pain that could have stopped me from moving on. I had come home! We stood there looking out over the Pemigewasset Wilderness and saw no sign of man's interference with Nature… no roads… no buildings. It was breathtaking. The trail went on as far as we could see behind us as well as in front of us, and the ridge on which we stood was only a few feet wide. On either side were drop-offs plunging into valleys of greens, reds and yellows. The sight inspired no fear, just awe! I do not know how long we stood there in absolute silence allowing our minds and hearts to be at peace, but eventually a gentle breeze came up from the valley and brought me back to earth.

We continued on to Mount Lincoln. Hiking along a ridge is, if you pardon the expression, a peak experience. You are afforded a panoramic view, and the actual hike requires very little of you after you attain the crest of the ridge. That day I coined a phrase that Dr. Wilton, a local Podiatrist, threatens to put on my tombstone: IT WILL BE BETTER WHEN WE REACH THE RIDGE!

We hiked along this beautiful path with just our thoughts, the rich brown rocks, and the views of the valleys below. The greens of the trees seemed to turn from lime to dark green as clouds blew overhead and caused shadows on the ground below. Since the gentle breeze had become a gentle wind by that time, we did not linger at the top of Mount Lincoln very long. We hiked ahead to a more sheltered spot. There, Carla and I pooled our lunches and shared a meal that could have been catered by the Ritz! Cold meats, cheeses, grapes, peanut butter cookies and juice never tasted so good. After lunch, wrapped in silence, we sat—simply enjoying who we were and all that was around us.

The trail from Mount Lincoln to Mount Lafayette is rather steep, but not as exhausting as some other trails. I think that this is because of the tremendous views all along the way. At the summit of Lafayette, we met several hikers who had spent the night at Galehead Hut and were headed towards the Flume. We were happy to inform them that their way would be easy. We shared a few stories and snacks and separated to go our own ways. The descent was torture! After a few jarring boulders, Carla put on knee supports and I tried to tie bandannas on my legs to prevent my knees from turning with each impact. I was never to hike without supports again. As we were climbing up a gully just before arriving at the Hut, we were assaulted by a frightening sight. We heard a roaring sound and looked up to see a huge black plane flying within spitting distance to the ground. You could almost read the name pin on the pilot! I was sure he was going to crash... but suddenly the plane and the sound were gone. We were informed that our military was using the White Mountains to test planes for Terrain Flight... so much for unspoiled beauty!

Greenleaf Hut, a single building with two bunk rooms, is a beautifully situated and isolated cabin overlooking Eagle Lake. We were disappointed to see that, due to drought, the lake was

Hey, Lady!

reduced to a swampy area. Like all of the huts, it is co-ed sleep wise, but has gender-separated bathrooms. Greenleaf is known for its unusual sunsets viewed from the back of the cabin. Every night at a designated time, all work stops and the crew exits the building. All who follow are treated to a memorable sunset. As we stood there waiting for something to happen, we were astounded by a flash of sunset reflected from mountain to mountain to mountain… a phenomenon. We could understand why some people return here over and over again just to view this two-minute event.

That evening we met and became friendly with two diverse gentlemen. One man resembled Roy Rogers in language and manner, while the other was out trying to find himself in the mountains. Roy Rogers was awaiting the arrival of his son who had taken a year off from college to hike the Appalachian Trail from Georgia to Maine. He arranged to meet his son to supply him with food, clothes, and other necessities at various drop-off points along the way. It was touching to see the pride of the father matched by the gratitude of the son when they met at the shelter. The young man even took the time to review Carla's and my packs and he gave us some advice about how to lighten our loads.

After supper, I was given the opportunity to indulge myself in another favorite pastime. I did some things learned in a Psychic Development class. A little palmistry, a few energy transfers and we went full swing into psychometry. Psychometry is holding an object and letting the mind wander to pick up facts about the object's past or about the owner of the object. All who wanted to participate had to put an object in one of the breadbaskets and then pull out a different object. The objects ranged from a toothbrush to a very expensive looking watch. After quietly holding the object for a time, each person just began to talk in a free-association manner about the object and its owner. It was amazing how accurate the people were. It almost spooked the spooker! After a second round, the Crew reluctantly told us that the lights would be put out in a few minutes. It seems that the hut is limited to only so many hours of fuel per night, and we had used about two night's worth.

The morning dawned with the usual mist and rain, but inside we were warm and contented. Breakfast was a wonderful meal and the crew outdid themselves to make us comfortable. It was difficult to leave the hut. We put on our rain gear and all too soon were swallowed up in the bushes that hid the hut from our view. Fortunately, Mother Nature decided to smile upon us and less than an hour later, we were stripping down to shorts and tee shirts again. The views down the trail to the road were mostly hidden by limbs and brush. At one spot, however, we found a huge boulder jutting far out over the valley. Fighting a feeling of vertigo, I held onto a young Spruce and looked down into the valley. I said a prayer to thank God for allowing me to be back up in my mountains again.

We arrived at the road in the latter part of the morning and found our way back to the car. There was plenty of time to drive to Conway to shop for a few of the things that the young man had suggested. I truly enjoyed Carla's company and we shared more hikes in the next few years—all of which were fun. When things became rough for me, Carla was one of the people who came back into my life to help me keep hiking. I will never forget that—ever!

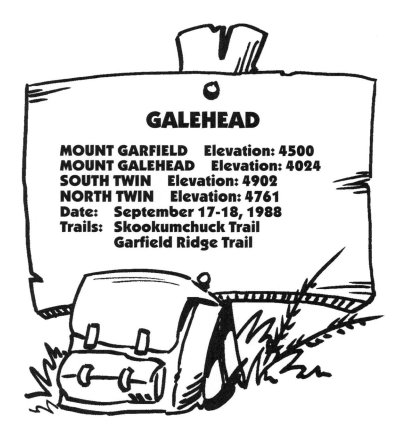

GALEHEAD

MOUNT GARFIELD   Elevation: 4500
MOUNT GALEHEAD   Elevation: 4024
SOUTH TWIN   Elevation: 4902
NORTH TWIN   Elevation: 4761
Date: September 17-18, 1988
Trails: Skookumchuck Trail
           Garfield Ridge Trail

THE IDEA was basically a good one, full of promise and fun. I had spent my 1988 hiking season thus far with my daughter's Girl Scout troop camping and hiking some local trails such as Chocorua and Hedgehog Trail, a hike that my good friend Dr. George Patten, had helped design as a student at UNH. Our hospital's excellent Activities Committee posted an announcement that a Beginner's Hike was in the planning stages and that they were looking for people who might be interested in joining the fun. Nancy and Carl Seavey had convinced Pat

Simms, a coworker in the X-ray department, and her husband, Jim, to go with the group. Since we were all hiking parallel climbs, but never together, she suggested that Mike and I join them. Mike had prior commitments, but I was very interested. The only problem I had was that I was a slow hiker and feared that I would be embarrassed by my slowness in a group situation. A planning meeting was held at Carol and Bob Sharer's home and I was hooked. The Sharers were to be the group leaders for this venture. The chosen mountains seemed to involve quite an elevation, but that did not seem to be a problem to the planners. I expressed a concern that I would not be able to keep up, or, God forbid that I would slow everyone else down, but this was not considered a problem by the others. We would just enjoy the scenery more at a slower pace. Carol and Bob were the pros on this hike. They had even climbed in the Grand Tetons Mountains of Wyoming. We listened intently as they outlined what they felt we needed to carry and voted on the plan as presented. There was even a slide show following the planning meeting. I was feeling that this climb would be another peak experience. Dr. Ed Yeganeh and Geoff Patten from the hospital enthusiastically committed to go.

We spent the night before the hike in a time-share house that Carol and Bob owned with other hikers and skiers. It was a huge old Bed and Breakfast with many rooms and surprisingly comfortable beds. I realize now that we did not stay there so that we could have an early start, as much as the fact that we had no where to run when the final plans for the hike, mileage, and time expectations were discussed. The words "Boot Camp" and "Forced March" sprung into my mind! We spent a relaxed evening reviewing everyone's pack and discussing the contents. My pack was selected as having too much stuff in it… my beloved knee and ankle supports were a prime example of what

Hey, Lady!

could be eliminated. I did not take them out. Nancy had some hair gel and moisturizer that was hooted over… she left that in too. So much for bowing to the wisdom of the experts!

In the early hours of the morning we were awakened in time to shower before a communal breakfast. The talk centered on previous hikes, ventures into the wilderness, and the upcoming trails. After putting the house in order, we went into the cars and drove to the base of the Skookumchuck Trail. As we stood there, I looked around me and was filled with a feeling of unpleasant anticipation. Everyone there was over 5'10" and had legs up to their necks. I thanked the Lord that Geoff Patten was not in that category and felt more at ease until he put on shorts. I saw his calves… muscles! I knew I was in trouble. Two of the other hikers, Bob and Jim, drove off to park a car at the exit point where we planned to emerge from the woods the next day. During their absence, I suggested that since I was slow, I should start climbing on ahead, which I proceeded to do along with the Seaveys and Geoff. It was not long before the rest of the group passed me. My head was echoing my pulse and I knew that I had to slow down and pace myself if I intended to last the day. I set my own pace and the others went on alone after I assured them that the two men who had dropped off the car would soon be catching up and I would not mind having the trail to myself for a while. It turned out to be a fine and wonderful group to hike with. Everyone took turns hiking a bit slower than usual. Jim and Bob would sit back and let me hike ahead of them, and then catch up with me only to take another break to let me hike at my own pace. They were not in the least condescending towards my rather unorthodox climbing methods. I do give a new definition to the word slow! My favorite companion of the day was Carl. He waited for me at one of the junction points on the trail and set a pace that was easy, although challenging. We were able to talk and walk at the same time. He had had a lung collapse at one time in his life and assured me that he was more comfortable at this pace and that there was no hurry. He really relaxed me and I felt good about hiking with him. Carl and I arrived at the top of Mount Garfield in exactly guidebook time. The others had arrived about an hour before. We ate lunch and took time to take photos at the summit. A cold wind found us there, and I put on Gortex for the first time and fell in love with it. Another thing to always carry in my pack! My Gortex suit had been bought in a close-out sale. I laugh now when I see the photographs showing me with my Gortex tied up at the ankles with my daughter's purple shoe strings.

Happily the rest of the way to the Galehead Hut was along a ridge and the going was easy. As we checked in a gentle rain started. The crew informed us that it would only take about twenty minutes to get to the peak of Galehead Mountain, but most of the hikers were now tired—personally I think they had used all their energy running up the first peak. I asked, begged actually, Geoff to accompany me. At that point in time, I did not relish the idea of having to climb back up that trail to bag Galehead peak if I ever decided to finish the four-thousand footers. Geoff graciously agreed to accompany me. We carried only water between us and in our lovely Gortex rain gear, we set off alone to conquer the peak. There was not much to conquer. The top was marked by a small cairn and a small sign but no views. The reward for exerting the extra effort was seeing a beautiful deer grazing at the top. She was as startled as we were, but just sauntered off. When we arrived back at the hut, the rest of the group questioned why I had gone on to the top after seeming so tired and admittedly slower than the rest. I guess I just recover fast. Ed had a few choice remarks to make about how much easier hiking would be if I weighed less, but all in all, the group just teased me good-naturedly about my style.

Supper was a delight at the hut that night. We were all on a super-high from the climb and from the company. We had formed a cohesive group and were really getting to know and enjoy each other. After supper, the crew entertained us with a guitar and songs. Then I started to do a little Palmistry. It must be the thinner air of the mountains or some quirk of elevation, but the readings went extremely well. For some, it was revealingly accurate. During the readings, I came down with a cough that would not quit. Ed left us and came back with a small green bottle. He handed it to me and I felt like we were characters in some Alice in Wonderland scene. Ed was the Mad Hatter handing me, Alice, the bottle that says "DRINK ME". I felt much better shortly after. The readings continued. We began passing a bottle of D.O.M. Brandy around the group. Ed sat quietly watching me loose sensation in my lips and get drowsy. It seems that liquid codeine mixes very well with Brandy. I rolled off to bed and slept the sleep of the truly innocent, or the truly inebriated! I do not even remember turning over once.

The next day dawned clear as a bell. The sun was warm and the air was cool and crisp. It was an ideal day for hiking and we were all anxious to be on our way right after breakfast. Going downhill was my forte at that time and I was soon proudly out ahead of the rest of the group in the lead position. This was more to my liking. Alas, it was not to last. First the Sharers and the Sims joined me for a while, and then with a twitch of their long legs, left me alone on the trail. For a while I heard them talking in the distance, and then silence reigned. It was pleasant being alone for a while, but as with all good things, that came to an end when I did not see any trail markers and did not hear any sounds from the group ahead or the group behind. There is a penalty for marching at a different pace. I felt and tried to suppress the fear that I could have wandered off the trail. Where could I have gone wrong? There had been no trail intersections or trail signs that I had noticed. The idea of backtracking to the hut had no appeal to me whatsoever, but after waiting several minutes, I made the choice to do just that. I began the laborious ascent. God was kind to me. I had not gone very far when I recognized Nancy's voice in the distance. I have never been so glad to see a group of people in my entire life. We hiked along together to the summit of South Twin. The sunshine of the morning was a mere memory. We were being swallowed up in a fog bank. Fortunately for me, the others were still a bit stiff from yesterday's exertion and I was able to keep up pretty well until the base of North Twin appeared. By then, I felt I had used any energy reserves I had saved from childhood! Each step was a challenge. Carl stayed with me as a light rain started and we helped each other into our rain gear. It was not easy to do because everything stuck to everything else and just when we thought we had our rain gear set to snap, the wind would blow it around. Carl forced me to take the lead and to set the pace. I will always be grateful for Carl's support that day. He encouraged me by saying how he enjoyed going more slowly and promised to keep climbing with me... a promise that he has faithfully kept all these years! We did not stop at the summit at all, but continued on at a faster pace downhill. We joined the others in a short period of time. Fortunately, the weather changed for the better after we began our descent and we were soon back in summer clothes and enjoying the sun again.

We broke for lunch at the first point where Little River crosses the trail. I had packed hard-boiled eggs, cheese, teriyaki strips, and fruit. As usual, I had packed too much food and shared with the others. Ed had brought fresh tomatoes and they added a zest to the trail lunch. They were worth their weight in gold. We were able to take the time to wade in the stream and did so with great pleasure. Unfortunately, Carl had a slight accident at that point. He had not brought appropriate boots for the hike and suffered a slight sprain. I used the last "unnecessary" piece of equipment in my pack—an ankle support. I would bet that Carl and I enjoyed the hike down more than the others. We stopped to soak his ankle more frequently than necessary. We spent a lot of time just listening to the silences and the noises of the woods. It was a disappointment to leave the red squirrels preparing for the winter too soon to come, and the birds which had followed us on the way out. The sounds of the cars on the highway seemed to assault our ears.

By the time we left the shelter of the woods, Bob and Jim had left to pick up the cars and we soon found ourselves back in civilization and on the road home. Geoff graciously offered to drive part of the way home. I sat back and rested my head on the seat and thought over how nice the hike had actually gone. When I arrived home, I put the information about this hike in my journal and realized that I had actually climbed sixteen of the forty-eight four-thousand footers. For the first time I thought that there was a chance that I might actually join the Four Thousand Footers' Club... at least it was a goal and the *AMC Guidebook* became the resource for hike selections from that point on. As the 1988 hiking season came to an end, I resolved that in 1989 I would begin hiking as early as possible.

THE HANCOCKS

MOUNT HANCOCK NORTH
Elevation: 4403
MOUNT HANCOCK SOUTH
Elevation: 4274
Date: May 29, 1989
Trails: Hancock Notch
**   Hancock Loop**

IT WAS probably remiss of me to not mention one of my most difficult problems in hiking. I cannot cross streams with any amount of skill. Usually I stand like a complete unbalanced fool tottering back and forth on the boulders abutting the stream until someone either comes to my aid or yells loud enough to force me to make a move. It is not unlike a puppy trying to jump off the couch the first time. I have a way of pacing back and forth waiting for the waters to part so I can cross… or maybe I just expect the rocks to give some sign of

Hey, Lady!

which ones are not slippery as I watch hopelessly while some long-legged hiker just stretches across, keeping one foot securely set on the previous rock.

On the last hike of 1988 I managed to murder my wonderful gray hiking boots when, in a fit of pique, I surrendered to a primal urge to not fall, and walked into the water with the boots securely in place. Bob told me that I had just taken a year off the life of my boots, but at the time I really did not care that much and who was to know that they were so close to their demise. I went to check them out for my early season hike and the fabric crumbled. There was a moment of silence, then a trip to the local sporting goods store to buy a new pair.

The decision was a difficult one to make. So many claims, fabrics, colors, and names to choose from. It was impossible. I wound up with an expensive pair of brown leather boots which were guaranteed to eat up the miles on a hike. Great support and all. They were not as attractive or as comfortable as my old friends, but time was short and they needed to be broken in.

Mike proved to be a willing participant in the first climb of the season. It was nice to get out so early in the spring compared to the past few years. No one else was interested in going as they feared that the black flies would be murderous at that time. We armed ourselves with various bug repellents and off we went. The drive up Route 3 is not my favorite one, but it happens to be Mike's. We talked about the children. Michael was now in college, and Kristyn was just finishing high school. We stopped for coffee and muffins along the way and soon arrived at one of my favorite roads, the Kancamagus Highway. I love this curling road with all the scenic stops and vistas. One day in my dotage, I will hire a limousine and stop every twenty or so feet all the way up the road and all the way back. I will be served strawberries dipped in dark chocolate and sip sparkling

Hey, Lady!

cold white wine from a fluted gold glass. We all have our dreams! We parked the car at a viewpoint and backtracked to the start of the Hancock Notch Trail.

At first the trail was an easy one. We were able to walk beside each other and even to hold hands for a while. We had packed only one backpack between us with an extra canteen of water. We followed an old logging road for an hour or so. The only other creatures on the trail were some small brown birds that flitted ahead of us as we imitated their songs. We enjoyed their company. The true trail actually began with a stream crossing. Mike, (whose theory is that if you cannot cross a stream by yourself, you do not belong on the trail), was not inclined to give me a hand across, so I gamely leaped onto the nearest large boulder. As I stood there waiting for the waters to divide, I found myself slowly sliding into the stream. The bottoms of my boots were as slick as ice. Much to Mike's amazement I hot-footed it across the stream. I could not believe that a boot company would oil the bottoms of hiking boots! Mike did not believe me until I later stood on a rockface and slid around and down the side of the rock. It made the rest of the hike a bit intimidating.

Having read in advance that the South Link portion of the trail was very steep, we approached via the North Link. It was a good decision. We were afforded not only an easier trail, but many beautiful views as well. It was wonderful to be in the woods as they were coming to life. All the birds and forest creatures were scurrying about in the warm sun. Lunch was an unhurried affair for a change. Lunches on my previous hikes had to be rushed in order to keep up with the group or to assure our arrival at the peak in time to get down the mountain before dark. We were able to lounge about on the summit just enjoying each other and the distant view of the Sandwich

Range. We saw signs of trail bike tracks whenever there was a damp patch of earth, and we worried that we would run into someone going full-speed down the mountain. We never did, for which I was grateful. The only regret that I had about this climb was that we had not decided to camp out. The thought of camping out does not normally appeal to me, but this trail called out for it. There were several camps set up in totally lovely flat areas with nearby water supply. The people were just rising as we passed by and we had twinges of envy. The day passed quickly and we found ourselves at the loop junction all too soon. This spot marked the end of the trail in and the beginning of the trail out. I enjoy loop trails because they circle around back to the point of origin. We left the mountains behind with the intention of returning to camp there someday. We returned to the car in good hiking time. It was necessary for me to sit on the back of the car to clean myself off with the remainder of my canteen water as I had mud caked on my legs from ankle to thigh. Mike must have taken a different trail as he was virtually spotless. He was in such high spirits that he benevolently agreed to return along the Kancamagus to Route 16 and even let me stop and freeze myself to death by taking a pre-season swim at White Pond, our vacation spot. It was a perfect day!

CANNON MOUNTAIN

Elevation: 4100
Date: June 7, 1989
Trail: Kinsman Ridge Trail

THERE ARE times in life when one can freely question one's brain power. In retrospect, this climb was a prime candidate for me. I could not have done any more stupid things without guidance from a genuine fool! I was very anxious to do a hike, any hike, and tried to find a buddy to go with me, but to no avail. Most people were working and those who were not had other plans. I decided to go alone. The day broke with threats of rain and the weather reports were not promising for the mountains. Mike suggested that I postpone the hike for a week at which time he would be able to go with me. I remained determined to go. I dressed and left while the rest of the household slept.

The sky remained dark and threatening most of the way up Route 3, but I had hopes that the mountains would be clearer. It seemed very strange to be going hiking by myself and I admit that I had brought my charge card just in case it rained hard and I needed to abort my mission. I will even admit that the prospect of being alone with no one else to depend on seemed to become less attractive with each passing mile. I comforted myself with the realization that I had control of the situation and I could go as far as I wanted with my plan. My decision would not affect anyone but myself. I arrived at the tramway about nine o'clock in the morning. During the last half hour of my drive, the sky cleared, and the day was now ideal for hiking. I took this as a sign that all would be well. I had difficulty finding the base of the trail. After reading and rereading the *AMC Guidebook*, I managed to find a small sign by the wooded entrance. I took a really nervous deep breath, hitched into my day pack, and off I went on my first solo hike.

There was no one else in sight all the way to the top. Since it was early in the season, the people who do all the wonderful work clearing the trails in the Spring had not been up the Kinsman Ridge Trail. The steep trail was very difficult because several trees had fallen across the trail. I would walk a few yards and have to decide whether to climb over or crawl under a tree, and then progress slowly to the next blowdown on the trail. There was a certain cadence to the hike, though, and it was enjoyable in its own way. The flying insects were buzzing about, but not biting yet, so their presence added a steady drone to accompany the rapid beating of my heart. I was able to acquire several scrapes from the bark of the pines and a few splin-

Hey, Lady!

ters. The fact that I was alone did not seem to make much difference to me after I was on the trail. The blazes were placed in such a way that they were relatively easy to find. I enjoyed the aroma of the rich warm soil and the varied smells of Spring in the air. The pace was easy and it was not long before I could hear voices above me. I arrived at the summit only slightly the worse for wear. There is a nice viewing platform near the Tramway and I joined a family from Connecticut in looking over the highway. My pleasure at having climbed to the top by myself was dimmed by their asking me: *Hey lady! How did you get way up here?* They thought I was crazy, and told me tales of horror about hiking alone and about attacks by wild animals. My only consolation was that these folks, appearing to be in their late seventies, seemed to be terrified of the world in general. I left them at the platform and moved to the building by the Tramway. A Ranger was standing alone and I went over to say hello. He was full of information about the mountains and their history, especially recent history. We talked for a while before he dropped his bomb. Bears. There were verified reports of a pair of marauding bears nearby. I told him that I was on the trail alone and he just looked at me for a few moments in silence. He then stated that it should not be a problem as long as I were not in my menstrual phase. Uh oh! I deliberated on taking the Tramway down to the car.

Sitting by the trailhead, I tried to make up my mind whether to walk the trail back to the car or to ride the Tramway. Taking the easy way out seemed to be the only sensible thing to do and I got up to go back to buy my ticket. A large group of college students arrived at the platform at that moment and I overheard that they were heading down by the same trail that would take me back to my car. They were the answer to my prayer. Being young and enthusiastic, they would create enough noise and diversion to scare any self-respecting bear away. I started out a few minutes before they did and was soon passed by the first group of students. They cleared parts of the trail as they bounded down the path making my way much easier. I was passed by the last of the group just as we left the woods. In retrospect, I realize that I may have made the wrong decision. I am lucky that God protects fools and little children—especially the fools!

MOUNT MADISON

Elevation: 5367
Date: August 19, 1989
Trails: Great Gulf Trail
Osgood Trail
Valley Way

EACH OF the AMC Huts has a log book available for guests to write about his or her adventures on the trail. From the first time I entered a hut, I had read about the horrors of Mount Madison. There are volumes of these journals filled with stories of exhaustion, accidents, and of people making several attempts to conquer this peak. I had planned to save this mountain for last just in case I changed my mind about finishing the forty-eight hikes. Fate intervened in the person of Joe Wallace. Joe, Mike, and I, belong to a square dance club. We were talking at a dance when we mentioned hiking. It seems that Joe is an avid hiker. He then suggested that we join him on a hike that he would like to get out of the way. I blithely agreed and the die was cast. Joe called with the reservation information a few weeks later and the trip was scheduled for August. In addition to Joe Wallace, moral support was provided by my friends and hiking companions Carla Marvin and Carl and Nancy Seavey. Two friends of the Seavey's, Gene White and his son Ryan, also joined in this climb. We planned to go up the Osgood Trail which appeared to be the lesser of all the evil trails that go up to this peak.

Carla was very enthusiastic about the hike and by the time we met the others off the highway, I was champing at the bit to get my boots on and hit the trail. The day could not have been any better. The sun was shining, and there was a wonderful cool breeze to keep the heat down and the bugs away. When we met Joe at the assigned area, he gave us the news that the trail had been closed for repairs a few days before, and that he had selected a new trail that left from Dolly Copp Parking area. We all piled back into our cars and took off down the highway. It took quite a while to get ourselves organized, so Carla and I left the others behind and wandered off down the trail to get a head start. We had reviewed the map and knew that we had a long day ahead of us.

It was a long, arduous hike. I tried to remember everything Mike had told me about hiking. Do not look up ahead. Just keep putting one foot ahead of the other and look for opportunities to get quick breaks. This is called pacing yourself and is effective in conserving energy on a long hike. Psychologically, it makes it more difficult if you look up and only see constant elevation awaiting you. Ryan White had the advantage of youth for quite some time, but as the day progressed

Hey, Lady!

and the sun got higher in the sky, he ended up having others take item after item from his pack to lighten his load. I admire him for making the great effort to come along and attain this peak. It was a hard trail. Signs saying that we should not climb this trail unless in excellent physical condition appeared a couple of times. Once we made it out of the woods there were wonderful views. We were able to keep together and it was a pleasure to be with these people.

Everyone had been willing to get an early start to allow for frequent rest times, and all of us took advantage of them. It was the first time I removed my pack and physically rested myself during breaks. In the past, I had just needed to lean against a rock or tree and to sip water or munch trail snacks. On this hike, we actually timed breaks so that we would rest. Along with the beautiful views from the exposed part of the trail came huge boulders. I envied Carl's and Nancy's long legs. Carla and I fell further and further behind as we scurried down one side and then up the other side of the rocks while the Seaveys skimmed over the tops. The sight of the Cog Railways' smoke and the curling silver ribbon of the Mount Washington Auto Road up the side of Washington was always to our left as we climbed. We labored on for about three hours and took shorter, but more frequent breaks. Lunch time was to be a long rest stop for us and we stopped to share our lunches at a great gathering of boulders with a clear view of Mount Washington and Wildcat. We all looked tired, but exalted. We were working together towards conquering the mountain and we could see the end ahead. We knew that we would be at the top by noon or shortly thereafter. It was a wonderful realization!

The arrival at the summit was celebrated by a water/snack break and high-five handshakes all around. It had been a long and arduous climb and we were all thankful that the trials and tribulations we had read about from our predecessors had been avoided by the group. The hike down was deliberately slow to avoid falls or an uncontrolled descent. It is a particularly steep trail. We arrived at the Madison Spring Hut and settled in the bunk room. A short time later, as we sat looking out the window, we saw some people who had arrived just before us coming back from a short jaunt. They said that they had climbed to the summit of Mount Adams. It seemed like a good idea to us. It was like a scene from Heidi on the mountain top. We climbed along trying to be careful of the delicate Alpine flowers along the path. The brush on that exposed mountain is dwarfed and bent in strange shapes due to the wind and weather. This brush is called "krummholz" which is German for crooked wood. In a surprisingly short time, we arrived at the summit. We took a long, satisfying break at the top and took photographs of the scenery and of each other. One of the pictures I took was a view of the hut with the summit of Mount Madison behind it. I would like to enlarge this photo someday for a den wall. It is a great shot. We came back to the hut quite proud to have attained two peaks of such reputation in one day. We were surprised to find that we had climbed the wrong Mount Adams. We had climbed Mount John Quincy Adams instead of the official four-thousand footer. No one was too disappointed because we had had too good a time on the trail together.

The Madison Spring Hut was built in 1888 and was the first of the AMC Huts. It is one of the most difficult to reach and just getting there is an accomplishment. The crew at Madison have many ecological projects, and they were very willing to share their studies and findings. One of the experiments had been to gather electricity by use of solar panels. It was the only hut so far that did not depend on oil for the lamps, al-

Hey, Lady!

though they did maintain them for emergencies. It was nice to be able to stay up as late as we wanted. It gave all of us time to get to know the others in the hut. We were fortunate to meet a lady doing a Park Usage study. We were able to give suggestions about trail use directly to someone who would have input on future changes. She shared many stories before she moved on the next day.

As was to be expected, the day dawned wet. I believe that this is an unwritten weather law in the mountains. At breakfast, there was much discussion about how best to return to the cars. Some of the group wanted to go back the way we had come. Personally, I would have preferred to jump off the mountain rather than to climb up that steep path again. As the debate went on, I spotted a booklet telling of the AMC's Shuttle Service and decided that no matter what the others did, this was my way home. I would take the Valley Way out and take the shuttle to Dolly Copp and wait for the others there. It was a happy decision.

When I told the others, they all decided (too quickly, if you ask me) to join me on my decided course. The descent down Valley Way is a pleasant hike out. It is the trail of choice for the Crew to carry in the large packs of supplies for the hut system. The choice was a good one. We arrived at the parking lot at the base of Valley Way in very good time and enjoyed a ride on the shuttle. The driver was a young man with many tales to tell and he told them with true Yankee humor. We arrived at the Dolly Copp area much too soon to please any of us. The ultimate compliment was paid to each one of us as we agreed to call each other for future hikes. It had been a long, tough, and challenging hike and we had done it well by helping each other along.

THE OSCEOLAS

MOUNT OSCEOLA
Elevation: 4340
OSCEOLA EAST PEAK
Elevation: 4156
Date: August 30, 1989
Trail: Osceola Trail

THERE WILL probably always be one or two mountains that will stand out among the rest as ones that you would like to climb again. Osceola is one of mine. This hike was not my first attempt of this mountain. Mike and I had tried to do this peak in the latter part of the previous Fall but had decided to turn back because of snow and ice. It was probably the first wise decision that I had made about hiking. It was always hard for me to make the decision to turn back if we had gone over half way… even if health or safety was involved. The decision to

Hey, Lady!

turn back was the right one to make as we were slipping on ice and it had started snowing. Fortunately, the hike had been relatively easy for me and it was not a difficult choice to make to decide to repeat the attempt at a later date. Today was the day.

We arrived at the parking lot adjacent to the trailhead and were dumbfounded to see a doctor from our local hospital heading out on the trail. We really wanted to hike alone, and it was obvious that he, too, was seeking solitude. We gave him a significant lead time before we started on the trail. This proved to be a useless gesture for it turned out that this doctor was in spectacular shape and runs up mountains for sport. We had not even reached the halfway point when we met him on the way down.

Osceola does not have spectacular views most of the way up because the trail is in the woods. It does have wonderful Outlook points all the way up. It behooves hikers to take the time to stop because the views from these points are breathtaking. Mike was more than willing to take breaks along the way and the climb was a wonderful memory for us. Most of the trail is wide and you can walk comfortably without getting too close to the edge. The woods were warm and we saw many birds and squirrels. It was a beautiful sight looking from an outlook about three quarters of the way up. We looked out to see mountain ranges in many shades of green. The sun and the clouds made the trees look like a living painting as we watched like eagles from the high point.

Towards the top, Mike became restless and went on ahead. There are times when you hike too slowly in order to accommodate someone else's stride and you will tire easily. It is necessary sometimes to take off at your normal rate for a while to recover yourself. Within ten minutes I heard Mike yell that he was at the top. The last switchbacks on this trail were annoying to me, because just when I thought I was at the top, I found myself climbing again. We were aware that a fog had been coming upon us and were lucky that the view from the top was not obscured. We enjoyed a snack of fruit and granola bars at the top.

The decision to go on to the East Peak was an easy one to make. We had enjoyed the hike so far and aside from the frustration of the switchbacks, it had not been difficult. According to the *AMC Guidebook*, the distance between the two peaks is about an hour. We found that we went faster than guidebook time. There was only one difficult spot. There was a challenging chimney to climb down. A chimney is a steep narrow cleft in the rocks that goes straight down a cliff. In order to get up or down the chimney, it is necessary to brace your legs and hands against two sides of the rockface and scurry like a bug up or down. I was worried about that because Nancy Seavey had said that the chimney had caused her some concern, and aside from water crossings, nothing seems to bother Nancy.

The fog had lowered visibility considerably and Mike took the lead down. He took the pack that we shared and took a few steps only to disappear into the wispy clouds. I did not hear any loud thumps or screams of terror, and all too soon he called for me to join him. He waited a few minutes before threatening to come and get me. I began the descent on legs slightly steadier than rubber hoses. The chimney was not so bad after all, and the fog was a blessing in disguise. I could not see how steep it was and what I could not see, could not panic me. We embraced at the bottom and Mike told me how well I had done.

We went on and took a photo at the sign announcing the peak. It was in a cairn with no views. It was not a place to linger. The fog had cleared by the time we arrived back at the chimney. This was not in my best interest emotionally, but I wanted to seem brave and I opted to go first. It was remarkably easy and actually enjoyable. Talk about being surprised with yourself. I was tempted to go back down and climb up again. The trip down was just a pleasant walk. The way was marked well and the weather was as perfect as one could ask. We had almost arrived at the base of the trail when we met more people from Portsmouth. It was unbelievable to go so far into the woods only to run into two groups of people from home. They were going to do Osceola and come back down. I hope their day turned out as wonderful as ours had.

ZEALAND MOUNTAIN

Elevation: 4260
Date: November 8, 1989
Trail: Zealand Trail
**   Zealand Ridge**
**   Twinway**

THERE WAS not enough time to do another big hike this year, but the chance to just get out into the woods and walk around at a leisurely pace presented itself. I could not resist. Mike agreed that he would like to drive up and climb to the Zealand Falls Hut for a lunch, hang around the hut for a while and come down. We made plans to eat at a restaurant as a group on the way back. A wonderful end to the climbing season. The group was probably the strangest mix of people so far. Dr. Wilton, my friend from the hospital, had heard me talking about the hikes and had been wanting to join us and he had these two active friends that he wanted to have come along. My neighbor was hosting a foreign exchange student from Germany who had mentioned that he wanted to go to the White Mountains just to see them. She asked if he could come along and save her a trip. It seemed like a good idea. We left after having breakfast at home and picked up Andy, the student, across the street. He was a very nice young man about eighteen or so. He asked many questions on the way up and related stories about his country. He was a good person to have along. We joined the rest of the group at Jim's house. As we drove along, we learned that his friends, Don and Sandy, had just come back from a unique vacation. Running Camp. A dark curtain of doom began to descend. I took solace in the fact that the trail to the hut is an easy one, and not too much of a challenge. Even with runners' legs, these people couldn't get too far ahead. I relaxed.

We arrived at the base of Zealand Trail and found no problem with parking. We went through the usual pre-hike stuff about spreading out but keeping within yelling distance of each other. Don, Sandy, and Jim were off like a shot. I saw them disappear into the woods as I looked up from tying my second boot. Mike was putting on his pack. Andy was just waiting around for his hosting couple. We shrugged it off thinking that the gazelles would probably be wasted by the time they got to the hut, and then they would have to wait for us anyway. No problems here. It was a red letter day for me. The day was a beautiful one with optimal weather... cool breeze and plenty of sunshine. The hike was supposed to take about an hour and a half, yet we found ourselves at the rocky point that is over three-quarters of the way to the hut in under forty-five minutes. It was a record time for me as I usually hike at guidebook time or about half an hour or so added to it. I was proud, but tired. We met with the others at the hut. They were drinking cups of coffee and enjoying the views from the Falls. We picked up some coffee and went out to stand on the rocks in the middle of Zealand Falls and looked down at the majesty of the mountains with their last leaves clinging to the trees. The sky was a deep azure blue. It was wonderful. I stood there entranced by the beauty.

When I returned to the matters at hand (mainly beginning the descent and planning what to order for dinner), I noticed the others poring over the map. This did not look good. A group decision was made to go on to the top of Mount Zealand. I was very concerned about going on as I had paced myself quickly for the short term and did not know if I could muster enough energy to climb upwards. What the heck. I decided to start with the others, and if I needed to turn back, I would. To this day, I'm not sure if the hike up Zealand Mountain from the hut is actually as bad as I judged it to be that day, or if my perception was off. I remember the trail as being straight up with no relief. I managed to put one foot in front of the other and heave up each step along the way. I was terribly winded almost from the beginning of the trail. At one point, Andy offered to take my pack for a while to ease my burden. I foolishly refused his help! I even used the trees along the way to pull myself up. Finally, we reached a ridge and the hiking was much easier from then on. The rest of the ascent to Zealand was not bad, and when the others decided to go on to Mount Guyotte, I did not protest. Renewed!

Hiking along this ridge was one of the greatest walks in the mountains. There were wonderful gray jays otherwise known as Canadian Jays. They are so used to people in the area that they have no fear. At one rest stop I took out my trail mix and was holding my hand out to shoo a bug, when one of the birds landed to steal my M&M's. His action totally surprised me.

The plants at this elevation are all dwarfed and misshapen. Most only come below waist height—even the evergreens. The vegetation was brown and very stiff, as if dead, but it was very much alive. They still had a good number of berries for the creatures. We had to remember to walk on the trail. Up there, it seemed that it would not make much difference where you put your feet, but it is vital to the survival of the plants to keep off the vegetation. The trails were laid out with much thought to the ecology. As one ranger put it… each plant can probably stand to have a person walk over it once, maybe twice, before suffering an injury. Multiply that by the hundreds of people on the trails each year, and you see that it is a wonder that anything survives the human touch.

Ridge-walking is one of my favorite things to do, and the rest of the hike, including the descent, was a positive experience. It was probably the only time I have so completely lost track of the clock. We were rushed in our descent as it began to snow while we were at Mount Guyotte. Don and Sandy set a nice, though rapid pace to the hut and we separated again at that point to return to the car. The ride home was uneventful as the snow stopped when we finished our descent. Andy seemed glad to have been included; Don and Sandy had had a good hike, but said they preferred running; Mike was going to come again to share my hobby; and Jim wanted to be included on the list of folks to call for hiking buddies. All in all, it was a great day!

MOUNT WILLEY

Elevation: 4302
Date: June 27, 1990
Trail: Kendron Flume Trail

JULIE JACKSON has been a friend of mine since we became
Girl Scout leaders in 1977. Julie is a smoker and had limited
her hiking to the UNH Trail on Mount Hedgehog. She mentioned from time to time that she should not have skipped
hiking Mount Chocorua with us, and she was sorry to have
done so. When Spring arrived, she was a logical candidate to
ask to go along on the first hike of the season. Her pace is comfortably slow and erratic, much like mine, and we always have
a lot to talk about. She is a fun person and I always enjoy spend-

ing time with her. We planned to do Mount Willey as soon as the weather allowed.

Bugs and biting insects are one of the biggest annoyances on hikes. The man who places his unprotected arm in a box of hungry swarming mosquitoes advertising a bug repellent has nothing on this girl. I place my whole body at their dinner table quite often. I have tried almost every lotion/potion known to man and have discovered one basic truth. All of them work on some things, once in a while, and for a short duration! In my quest for the perfect lotion, I once tried putting a different brand on each extremity only to forget which type was on which limb... not that it mattered. I was still bitten unmercifully! I usually try to get the bath oil type which does not actually repel the insects, just manages to drown them so I have to remove their tiny corpses at the summit and again at the base. At least they die before they get a chance to bite! For this trip, I had some new things to try... dryer sheets pinned to the back of my hiking hat, and Vicks Vapor Rub on the soles of my boots. I was not quite sure of the rationale of the dryer sheet, but had heard that all the old fishermen were swearing by them. The Vicks sounded like a sure thing. The premise was simple and sounded reasonable. The vapors would rise up as I walked to form a protective cloud of menthol that would repel the bugs. Somewhere along the way, I had heard that bugs were attracted to human carbon dioxide, so if I sucked on menthol cough drops, they would not get in my mouth as I panted. It sounded good to me and I gamely decided to test all three methods on this trip.

Julie and I got up early and had breakfast at my house. We were able to get an early start and found ourselves at the Willey House Site before eight thirty. It was a pleasant drive up. At the base of the mountain, I applied the Vicks to the soles of my

Hey, Lady!

boots... sure that I had found the answer to the bloodsucking creatures. I gave Julie the option of trying it, but she wisely refused. She did take a dryer sheet. I pinned the sheet to my cap, and heard a chortle from Julie, who called me a dork! I guess those old fishermen are not daunted about looking foolish with these sheets dangling down their necks. Julie pinned hers to the inside of her neckline. Smart! At the first brook crossing I learned the error of my ways. The Vicks attracted and held on like super glue to pine needles, mud, acorns, and even small boulders. Worst of all, it would not wipe off. I even tried washing it off with a bandanna and water to no avail. I felt like I was hiking in high-heeled shoes! It was probably not too safe. We kept taking breaks to enable me to scrape off the residual goo all the way up to the waterfall. At that point, I found some Mountain Suds in the bottom of my pack and was able to wash the stuff off. So much for Vicks. The dryer sheet will remain ever a mystery. I do not know if they work, or not. On one of our frequent breaks, we checked on the sheets only to find tiny little wings and legs, but no bugs. With identical cringes, we removed the sheets. We never found any bug bodies.

One of the interesting points on this trail is the railway. It is necessary to cross this structure, but the real fun is under it. There is a crawl space under the tracks that is quite large and gives flight to the imagination. There were signs of both human and animal habitation. Julie and I spent some time there filtering through the stuff like amateur archaeologists making up survival stories. It was fun. We soon arrived at the beautiful waterfall. Julie decided not to go any further at that point. She chose to sit by the falls, relax, read a book, and smoke. She took off her pack and arranged her worldly goods as I went on my way. As she lay back to light her first cigarette, her lighter jumped out of her hand and threw itself into the rapidly flowing water and was whisked out of her grasp! Julie jumped to her feet in a tremendous effort to rescue the lighter to no avail. It rushed over the side and out of sight. She had to content herself with trail snacks and her book... and the waterfall. This trail gets an B for easiness to follow. It is well-marked and laid out with comfortably ascending switchbacks. I do not usually get any great urge to sing on the trails, much to the relief of the wildlife, but I did on this one. I remembered old camp songs, songs from the twenties and thirties, and even old religious hymns—in Latin yet. Ah, yes, it was a grand day. The trail had its difficult spots, none of them dangerous, just difficult. Before I knew it I reached the Ethan Pond Junction.

The rest of the hike was a matter of looking at my feet and pushing myself to move up the mountain. I ran into some people coming down the trail, and they agreed to tell Julie that I was almost to the top, and that the descent would be fast. I did not know how she was doing by then or if she would be worried. I was taking quite a long time, and from time to time I heard rumbles of distant thunder. I took some time at the top to munch on trail snacks and juice, and then came down. I reached Julie at the waterfall in about half the time it had taken me to hike up. She was reading and so quiet that I hated to disturb her. We had run out of survival stories about the railway, so we just hiked down and off the mountain. We arrived at the car, and were able to find a single match on a book under one of the carpets in the car. Julie was happy. She even agreed to do Mount Chocorua in the summer. I was happy!

MOUNT MONROE

Elevation: 5384
Date: July 11, 1990
Trails: Ammonoosuc
           Ravine and
           Crawford Path

IT WAS time for another hike and it was easy to select the next peak. It was Mount Monroe. Nancy Seavey had just finished this particular hike for the second time and had found it to be a good one to do. Climbing alone on these trails would not be much of a problem since many people use the area and I would not be totally alone. I arrived early in the morning and returned to the now familiar Ammonoosuc Ravine Trail sign. It was my third time on this trail. I was looking forward to a wonderful day. I hoped to arrive at the AMC Lake of the Clouds Hut before ten o'clock and rest for an hour before climbing Mount Monroe. I was comfortable about climbing on the trail and arrived even earlier than anticipated. The gentle breeze at my back had kept me cool and had made my climb easier. My break at the Gem Pool was the only one of any substantial time that I took. The rest of my stops were taken to retie my boots and to drink water. I needed to remind myself to rest. It was a great day for me physically. I felt strong.

The Lake of the Clouds Hut is the largest of the buildings in the Hut System. It is also one of the coldest. They have an open stairway to the basement area and the wind comes in most of the time. The Crew was wonderful as usual, and listened while I told them of my hiking plan. I felt assured that even if I were alone on the trail, I was not completely alone. I had a hot drink, packed my light pack, and went along my way. This hike will go down in history as the one that I felt the best on. I was not tired. I was able to go to Mount Monroe, Little Monroe, Mount Franklin, and all the way to Mount Eisenhower before turning back to the hut. I was enjoying the southern peaks. I took some fabulous photos of the area. The whole ridge is exposed, and fortunately the sky was clear at intervals allowing great views. I swear I could even see the ocean way off in the distance—a blue line on the horizon. The distant sights were incredible. Most of the terrain is nondescript... just brown hard rock and hard soil. There were some very low bushes about that may have been blueberry bushes, but I could not be sure. I guessed that if there were any berries this high, they would come quite a bit later than July. Just before I decided to turn back, I ran into a woman hiking with her Golden Retriever. The dog was wearing a pack that carried his water and a couple of dog treats. I could not believe it. I was not really sure how far I had gone and she told me that I was just below Mount Eisenhower. It is amazing how far one can travel when not exhausted. I turned back. It was easy to keep Mount Washington in view for most of the trip back. The views from the Crawford

Path are great. I took time to take the loop around Mount Monroe on the way back and spent more time trying to orient myself with a compass and map. Even after two classes, my skill in this area remains minimal!

On arriving at the hut, I became strangely cold. Even sitting in a sheltered area just outside the hut protected from the wind did not help, although the hot rocks were a comfort. I bundled up in my down sleeping bag in the bunk room for a while, also without much relief. It was good to go in to supper where I chose to sit between two substantial people to steal a little body heat! A bowl of hot soup and a hearty meal helped and it was off to the bunk room early for me.

The following day dawned surprisingly clear. I had decided to climb down the Ammonoosuc Ravine Trail with a psychiatrist's wife. Her husband had spent the day before yelling at her to keep up with him and their teenagers. We gave them a short head start and began at a good pace. We enjoyed the scenery, the brook, and talking about men in general and their expectations of us. All in all, for a stranger, she probably learned more about me than most of my friends know. The morning flew by. Amazingly, there were no bugs to bother us. We met her family at the Emerald Pool, and cooled our feet while they took off like jackrabbits. Carol seemed unconcerned about their abandonment of her. When they had disappeared, she turned to me, smiled sweetly, and dangled the car keys. They would not go far without her! We started across the footbridge and returned to the business at hand. We arrived at the bottom of the trail where her husband sat waiting, and she was soon on her way back to Rhode Island. I, feeling the warm glow of accomplishment, went to the railway station where I bought a new shirt, locked myself in the bathroom and proceeded to take a shampoo and a sponge bath.

JEFFERSON–ADAMS

MOUNT JEFFERSON
Elevation: 5712
MOUNT ADAMS
Elevation: 5774
Date: August 18, 1990
Trails: Sylvan Way,
Randolph Path,
Gulfside Trail, Valley Way

WE WERE able to get a very early start on this climb and met everyone, all square dancers from our club, at the base of the trail before seven-thirty, a record for most of us! Rachel Wallace was not sure about her ability to hike, but I assured her that I was not a marathon hiker like her husband Joe. We would do just fine together. We were out to have a nice hike. There was some confusion at the beginning about the best approach to the summit. After discussing the possibilities with Jack Hill and

Hey, Lady!

Dana Wells, Joe selected the Sylvan Way. We spread out over the trail within five minutes with Rachel and I bringing up the rear. Rachel is a strong hiker, but is overshadowed by Joe who has legs that do not quit. She and I set a good pace. We were going slow enough to keep up a conversation some of the time while respecting each others' need to breath and be quiet at others. It was a pleasant morning with no biting bugs to plague us along the way. We were not making very good time, but the trail was very steep and difficult. It was necessary to take frequent breaks just to keep our pulses below two hundred. Even Mike, who tries to slow his pace to accommodate mine, could not manage today and soon left Rachel and me to go hike alone. We met with everyone at the Gray Knob Shelter. We explored around the area for the promised water supply and filled up the canteens. Lunch was a rather hurried affair and it was during that break that I made a bad decision. The rest of the group was going to skip climbing Mount Jefferson and go directly to Mount Adams. I was pretty sure that I did not want to repeat the trail to get to Mount Jefferson on another day and wanted to go on to climb Jefferson as planned. Mike agreed that it was best for me to go on and I put my pack on expecting him to come with me. He had not agreed that it was best for him. He chose to omit Jefferson.

The path to Jefferson was relatively flat and I was able to keep up a pretty even and fast pace. The terrain on the trail was similar to the rock formations at our beaches on the Seacoast and I skimmed across them with a feeling of comfortable familiarity and confidence. I came upon The Perch in record time and took a short, though unnecessary break at that point just to sit there for a couple of minutes and enjoy the view. I regretted not taking the camera with me. Mike had it. I joined a few Canadian couples in the ascent of Mount Jefferson but did not tarry long at the top. The afternoon was swiftly passing and I had a long way to go.

The day was extremely dry and a warm breeze was not helping my situation very much. My water supply was running low as I had used quite a bit on the Mount Jefferson climb. I could sense dehydration starting and used my water sparingly. There was supposed to be a spring along the trail somewhere between the two mountains and I hoped that I would find it soon. The terrain was similar to the one I had had such an easy time on earlier in the day, and I began the method of walking that I had learned in the Girl Scouts. This consists of jogging about fifty paces and then walking fifty paces. It is supposed to enable one to go long distances faster without becoming exhausted. It did make the going faster, but thirstier. I missed the spring, but found several puddles of water to soak my bandanna in. I tied it around my forehead to give me some protection and moisture. I found myself at the base of Mount Adams much sooner than I had anticipated.

At the trail junction, I made another wrong decision. I decided to climb over Mount Adams instead of circling around the mountain and joining the others of the group at the Madison Spring hut. My reasoning was simple enough. I did not want to have to climb all the way up here again, and I had already climbed the wrong Mount Adams once before. I was here, and it did not look too hard a climb from where I stood. I would probably miss the soup course at supper, but I would have accomplished climbing two impressive mountains in one day. There was plenty of daylight left. Mike knew what I was doing. If there were a problem, he would come after me. All that reasoned out, I took my first steps up Mount Adams. The hike up to the top of Mount Adams was actually quite easy as I enjoy that type of terrain. The boulders are spread out and it was easy to scurry up them. I kept up a good pace and soon found myself at the top trying to straighten out the sign designating the summit of the mountain. A couple of bolts were missing and the poor sign was upside down. I could not fix it. It took some time to figure out which direction to go to get down the mountain to the hut. As I stood there, the wind suddenly shifted. I felt myself being lifted up.

The next thing I knew, I was lying face down on some rocks, not knowing how I had gotten there—not a comforting feeling. There was a precipice just in front of me. With grim amusement I noted that if my breasts had not been caught in a ledge, I would have shot down the cliff. I could not feel my left arm and only touched the shoulder when I tried to find it. At first I thought it had been ripped off, but found my arm tucked up under the pack—numb, but still there. I edged back up and took some time to assess the damage. There was obviously something wrong with my left arm and hip… probably just pulled. I was able to fix that by stretching them slowly and gently. I had plenty of scratches and took some time to pour saline from the first aid kit over them to remove the lichen and dirt. Since the lichen on the rocks appeared to be moving, I was pretty sure that I had received a concussion. I was alive and mobile and there was not anyone around to help, so I began a slow and painful descent. I found myself talking to myself most of the way down as if I were a neutral third party to this whole mess. Most of the way consisted of sitting down, stretching both legs out to get a foothold and then easing my body down to sit and repeat the process. Any time I had gained earlier was swallowed up by the method I was forced to maintain. I could not look at the rocks without having the sensation of seasickness. For some reason, I became fixated on supper at the hut. I could just taste the food and wanted nothing more in life than to get there in time to eat. It was an obsession. I could not think about anything else and if other thoughts entered my brain, they did not last but a minute. God was on my side as I finally reached level ground. Supper faded into the background and all I wanted was to get to Mike.

A few hundred feet short of the hut, I ran into some people who put me into a state of confusion. I thought at first that I was dreaming. They were all dressed in white and had startling blond hair and light blue eyes. Their brightness hurt my eyes. They were beautiful. It did not compute in my muddled brain how they could have climbed this hellish mountain and still be clean. I was frightened by them and just wanted to get past them to the safety of Mike and the hut. They remarked about how hurt I was. As I stood staring at them, they seemed to become aware of my anxiety. Smiling, they parted to let me go past them. As I walked past their outstretched arms, I lost my negative feelings about them and felt warm and no longer afraid. We exchanged sincere smiles and I walked towards the hut. Strangely enough, I never saw them again either at supper or on the trail. I have never figured out who they were. Some people insist that they were angels and some say they may be members of a religious group. I think I may never know for sure, and somehow that is all right. Mike met me outside the hut with the hug I needed to be all right. He took my pack and helped me to the bathroom where I washed off the blood and cleaned up. I had one heck of a goose egg on my forehead and was glad the bandanna I had worn had kept my head from being badly cut. I was able to dress warmly and joined the group for the supper that had helped me make it down the mountain.

My streak of bad luck was not to end just yet. It seemed a group of hikers had brought a few bottles of Jack Daniels along and took them outside in the evening to indulge themselves.

Hey, Lady!

One of the men passed out and his friends left him alone without a flashlight. When a thunderstorm awakened him after midnight, he was somehow able to find the hut, but not the door. He ran around the building screaming and pounding on the walls. I heard him, but figured that it was either my imagination, or that if this was real, the crew would take care of it. He appeared at the window beside my bunk accompanied by a flash of lightning. I almost flew off the bed with fear. Shortly thereafter, he stumbled in and fell beside my bunk with his head on my pillow. I gagged on the smell of old liquor on his breath. Mike seemed to find the situation amusing and that made me furious! I climbed up to the crews' quarters and asked for assistance. They also found it funny, and I was left in a cold fury alone in the dining room, my bunk occupied! I pulled my sleeping bag free and wrapped it about myself to get what rest I could at the table. Mike came to get me a couple hours later when he saw the man go to his own area. I fell into bed to sleep soundly until breakfast.

We were fortunate that Mother Nature had spent most of her energy that night and we were blessed with good weather in the morning. I was still slightly nauseous but not too sore and we went out the Valley Way Trail to our cars. Valley Way is such a nice trail—I wished we had taken it up! We headed down to Route 16 where I was able to do a little shopping for patches and pins of the hut system on the way home. It was not the best hike that I had taken!

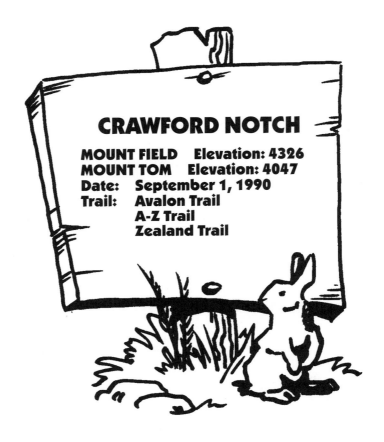

CRAWFORD NOTCH

MOUNT FIELD Elevation: 4326
MOUNT TOM Elevation: 4047
Date: September 1, 1990
Trail: Avalon Trail
A-Z Trail
Zealand Trail

JIM WILTON had been asking about going on a hike since early spring, but could not get free until now. Jim's wife, Tracy, arranged for a baby-sitter so she could join us this time. Geoff Patton, a co-worker at the hospital and his cousin Bruce were also planning a hike in the White Mountains for this particular weekend. It seemed like a good idea to hook up the two groups and go together. We mentioned it to Vicci Lamb, the receptionist at our dentist's office and she decided to come along with her friend, Robert Gigliotti, for part of the hike.

Hey, Lady!

They intended to leave us before we went to Zealand Falls Hut for the night. Our plans were set. The day started early, as gorgeous a day as one could pray for. We were scheduled to meet in the hospital parking lot by six-thirty, but Jim and Tracy were delayed. I was a bit concerned when they showed up because they looked like a couple of professional military persons. They were dressed in matching fatigues with Army backpacks and canteens. I could envision a long fast hike ahead of me. Fortunately, I was wrong. It was a great hike!

We arrived at the parking area by Saco Lake and prepared to hike. We took quite a bit of time getting our acts together. Finally Mike and I just started off. It was one of those days that you could spend the whole day getting ready and never get moving. We decided to begin up the Avalon Trail. This trail starts off relatively flat and the elevation sort of sneaks up on you when you least expect it. The trail is not the easiest to follow either. According to the map, we should have crossed the stream only twice, but we kept zigzagging back and forth. We would walk just so far and run out of trail markers. There would seem to be a good trail across the stream, so we would cross over only to find that the new trail only went a few hundred feet. We would have to back track or cross the water again. When the rest of the group caught up with us, we spread out on both sides of the water to find the right trail. For most hikers, this would not be a problem, but it was a major undertaking for me. Thank God Tracy was not a stream jumper either. We gave solace to each other at each crossing. Tracy was lucky because Jim had decided to carry all the weight of their gear, which left Tracy with only the canteen to balance. Just after the last stream crossing, the trail took a turn for the worse. It became very steep and ragged. I could tell that I was really out of shape and each step was a struggle. The others went on ahead when I explained that I would do better left alone to set my own pace without having to worry about holding them back. We agreed to meet at the base of Mount Avalon.

After much heaving and heavy breathing, I caught up with the others. They decided to climb Mount Avalon to get the view from the top. This is one of the best views in the mountains. It has the perfect perspective to view the highway and the Presidential Range across the way. I regret to say that I did not join the others. I felt I could use the time to forge on ahead and build up my speed a little. There was still a bit of elevation to go before attaining the peak, and I had developed a good cadence for myself. I did not dare to loose it. The rest of the group caught up with me as I was climbing up Mount Field. I admit that I was a little jealous about missing the great view they had seen, but I had made the right decision. I was rested by my pace and achieved the peak without being overly fatigued. The view was quite good from this vantage point, too, although not as dramatic.

We had lunch at the top. Jim had brought along a selection of rations, or MR80s. We all shared in the meals. There was a turkey one, a stew, and a mystery meat in sauce. The packages also had crackers and cheese as well as a different dessert in each package. We agreed that they should be set in hot water for a while before eating. For most of us, it was a first experience with Army Field Food. When I heard how many calories the Army puts into each bag, I decided my intake of these meals would be limited! We also lunched on fresh grapes from Vicci, cheese that I had provided, and crackers from about four packs. It was a delightful meal. We relaxed for several photos after the meal and lay about catching a few of the sun's fall rays. As with all good things, lunch break came to an end, and we started along the way to Mount Tom. The trail to Tom was

Hey, Lady!

easy and most of it seemed to be downhill. We arrived in a relatively short time. I was most fascinated by watching Vicci hike. It was not until I asked her how she managed to keep up such a good pace that I learned that she is a ballroom dance instructor. She is quite short and thin, but she is one strong hiker! I was impressed. Our friends, the Canadian Jays, showed up at this point to share our trail snacks. Geoff was particularly enthralled by the creatures who would land on his hand to feed without fear. Their tiny feet and light bodies were quite a contrast to our parrot, Maya. They followed us with an occasional raucous cry if we did not feed them often enough. We tried not to over indulge them so that they would not be in trouble when the winter months came and the human food suppliers stopped visiting.

Vicci and Bob left us before we started up Mount Tom. They were on the Avalon Trail at this point which would lead them back to his car. The rest of us took a few minutes to conceal our bags in the woods at the base and took only one pack between us to the top. Without packs, it was a simple walk to the peak. Using a pair of binoculars, we could see Zealand Falls in the distance. Jim tried, without much success, to show me a new and easy method of using a map and compass that he had picked up in the National Guard. It was useless for me, but the rest of the group spent some time picking out the various peaks around us. It was interesting.

The trail from Mount Tom to Zealand Falls looked very flat on the map, but it was not. It was a long, if not overly difficult trek. Everyone kept wondering if we were getting closer. I did not remember seeing too many trail signs and became a bit concerned about our direction on several occasions. I was also concerned about the number of huge moose tracks. We were relieved to find a pond at one point that we assumed was the end of Mount Field Brook. It was more of a boggy area, but since nothing else fit that description on the map, we took heart. We were rewarded finally with the junction of our trail with Zealand Trail and soon found our way safely to the hut. It was a good hike, and fun.

Our stay at the Zealand Falls Hut was a pleasant one. Jim and Tracy settled in the late afternoon sun on a hammock that Jim had hauled up, and the rest of us sat beside, or in, the Falls. The scenery was lovely. Such a nice fall day. When the weather began to get colder, we huddled together on the porch to watch the sun set and the moon rise. The only mishap was when I tried to show Jim my new head lamp and blinded him for about five minutes. Dinner was a filling meal of chicken and stuffing with potatoes, salad, vegetables, and breads. There was cobbler for dessert. We returned to the porch to enjoy the stars and the quiet. The sky was like black velvet and the stars sparkled like a thousand eyes looking down. It was difficult to leave the serenity of the porch to retire for the night. One by one we left to go to the bunk rooms for a long and well earned sleep.

In the morning, after a wonderful breakfast, we took the Zealand Trail to the waiting cars and car pooled back to Saco Lake. As most of the group slipped into comfortable shoes or slippers for the ride home, Bruce and Geoff added tents, more clothes, and food to their packs to go off on the second lap of their adventure. They were heading out to climb Mount Jackson. I can not say I envied them at all as I climbed into the car and melted into the seat. It had been a long, satisfying hike!

Hey, Lady!

MOUNT ISOLATION

Elevation: 4005
Date: October 10, 1990
Trail: Rocky Branch Trail
Isolation Trail
Davis Path

IT WAS late in the season to consider camping, but when Nancy and Carl suggested it, we agreed to go without any hesitation. Mount Isolation is one of the mountains that people save for last because it is as isolated as its name suggests. I read in the papers from the AMC about day hikes to this mountain, but those poor people must run all the way. I do not believe that I would make it out before midnight! No matter, we intended to take our time and camp out. It was my first camping trip without a horde of Girl Scouts and I was really looking forward to an adult trip. At a planning meeting, Jim asked if he could bring his son along. Sean was in second grade, and I hesitated, not knowing how to say no without losing a friend. I am glad that I could not, because Sean turned out to be one of the special children of this world. He hiked along without a single complaint and certainly beat me at Stream Crossing 101! He was a real trooper and was to join us on a few other hikes as time went on. I never hesitated about his coming along again.

Rocky Branch Trail is not a difficult hike, although it is certainly a long one. We walked along enjoying the silence of the woods for most of the first hour or so. Jim and Sean were in the lead so that Sean could set the pace, and the rest of us were very pleased with the speed. We took a break for an early lunch just before Engine Hill. Nancy had packed hard-boiled eggs for us to share, and we blended those with deviled ham, various cheeses and breads and sweets. It was a nice lunch even if we were perched on a hill. Carl and Nancy had a reflector blanket that acted like a sled if they both shifted weight at the same time. They provided a bit of comic relief for lunch time.

My trouble began at the Shelter No. 2 area... stream crossings! The first one was a winner. Rapidly flowing water and wide-spread, slippery-looking boulders are the stuff of my nightmares. I stopped like a rabid dog at the edge. Mike wandered off downstream to find his way, and I watched enviously as Jim and Sean crossed. Jim is about 6'2" and it seemed to be so easy for him. Nancy, my soul sister, stood frozen to the spot with me. We were duplicate ice sculptures. Carl crossed and came back for Nancy. I followed on her heels. I prayed that she would make it for if she did not, I would fall in after her! I made it to the next to the last boulder before reaching shore. I was stuck. I could not go back and I could not go forward. I knew that if Mike made it back upstream before I got to shore, he would yell, but I could not get the courage to jump the three feet or so to the last rock. Mike feels that if you cannot handle situations in the woods, you do not belong in them! This was definitely a situation. Carl came to my rescue. He positioned himself back onto a rock and told me to jump. He would catch me and then step back to shore. The last jump was only a couple of feet for me to do alone. He sounded very sure of himself so I built up my reserves of courage, balanced my pack, rocked back and forth to gain momentum and literally threw myself at Carl. He caught me all right—right about chest level. My forward motion carried us both over into the stream. One thing hikers try to avoid is wet boots, so both of us were scrambling to keep our feet out of the water. In the process, I was straddling Carl's chest, holding his head under water at times. He was struggling not only to keep his boots dry, but to avoid drowning. We were a mass of legs, arms, and heads. Nancy was laughing so hard she had tears pouring down her face. She later remarked that if she had had a camera, she could have taken us to divorce court.

I finally sacrificed a boot and got off Carl. I looked up to see a very embarrassed husband standing on shore. Once on solid ground, I became aware of blood running into my socks, in fact, quite a lot of blood. Jim, a podiatrist, began to look for the wound somewhere on my leg. When the cut was discovered on my elbow, he remarked with great humor that he did not do arms, only feet! I was taken care of very professionally in spite of the fact that I had wounded the wrong part and promised that if I acquired another injury, I would try for my foot. The incident would have probably been quickly forgotten if it had been an isolated one, but I tend to repeat mistakes. Apparently Carl has the same trait. I made it across a couple streams on embarrassed energy until we arrived at another mammoth one. I went into my hesitation waltz at the edge of the stream and Carl, only slightly more reluctant this time, came to my aid. This time, he came back for me and reached out his hand to guide me across to the last boulder. He guaranteed me that he knew what had gone wrong the first time, and assured me that it would not happen again. He lied! Over we went. This time, I put both feet down. I had to change into my sneakers until my boots dried out. Mike was so angry at my stupidity that he did not talk to me for about a mile.

We were able to arrive at our campsite without any more accidents and good humor was restored. Our site was in a small gully with the remains of a huge fire circle in the center. Water was a short distance down the trail. We gathered enough for two meals and everyone helped set up the campsite. The three tents were quickly erected. It took a remarkably short time to accomplish a lot of things. Since it was still early, we decided to go climb to the peak rather than wait until morning as we had originally planned. I felt badly for Sean who had just settled in to rest, but with only a token grumble, he joined us. The hike to the top was not overly difficult, but we were tired from hiking all day. We saw a few tents set up in weird locations along the way. One was actually perched in a rock ledge slab. We attained our goal by about six o'clock, the Seavey's in the lead, followed by Mike and me. We took a fabulous photograph of Jim and Sean as they bagged their first peak together. They were justifiably proud! It was a shared feeling of accomplishment.

Due to a slight wind, we made only a small fire and gathered around it to cook and to enjoy the company. It was a pleasant evening. Sean nodded off about eight o'clock and the rest of us followed at about ten. The wind died down and the night was warm enough for us to be able to sleep on top of our sleeping bags. With the zipper of the tent open, I lay awake for a long

Hey, Lady!

time watching the darkness and enjoying being in my mountains. I even ventured away from the campsite to sit quietly in the moonlight by myself for a while. A treasured moment!

In the morning we awoke to the smell of coffee cooking on the fire. Jim had the brew ready by the time we donned our sweats. Nothing tastes better than brewed coffee in the mountains. We enjoyed two pots before we got into any serious eating! With much clowning around, we packed our tents and started down the trail toward our cars. The stream crossings were much better from this side and I had no further water-wrestling events with Carl. We made much better time on the way down, and I became aware that the trail had a definite grade to it. It had been uphill all the way to the camp. No wonder we were tired.

We stopped at a barbecue pit on the way home to fill our cholesterol quotas for the year and enjoyed an uneventful ride home. I would repeat this hike in a heartbeat!

MOUNT MOOSILAUKE

Elevation: 4802
Date: May 25, 1991
Trails: Gorge Brook Trail
          Glencliff Trail

THIS PAST fall and winter, I decided to experiment with exercise. I had been getting short of breath on the trails, and my legs lacked the stamina to attain any peaks. The hospital offered a new program called Fit for the Future. It involved aerobics and a combination of the Nautilus and exercise machines at the Jackson Gray building, which is associated with the hospital. I became obsessed with the program and started going every other day without fail. Nancy, Carl, and Carla joined the

Hey, Lady!

program also and we spent many painful, breathless moments on the machines, dreaming about how wonderful and easy climbing would be after all this exercise. Personally, I secretly hoped that it would not work so that I would not have to keep it up. The Stair Stepper was my nemesis and I worked at it until I could finally get up to fifteen minutes at level three, maybe four, if the computer was being nice to me. Everyone else had started out at that level, but I refused to be daunted by this and continued to go to the building three times a week and eventually added aerobics. The promised weight loss never happened, which did not surprise me at all, but I did feel stronger about my legs and noticed a difference in my lung power. I did not get short of breath on the stairs anymore. At last winter passed and climbing season began.

Mike agreed to take me on the first hike of the season. We later agreed that this mountain was the most pleasant one that we had done. The folks in the Physical therapy Department were right. My legs were great on this hike! We rose early and were able to find a restaurant open for a light breakfast. We were on our way. We were lucky to get an early start as the sights from this mountain are irresistible and we would have been in the woods until after dark if we had not planned our time. We found the Ravine Lodge without too much difficulty and were pleased that the road in was uphill, promising a few feet less elevation for the climb. Every foot counts at times. I hoped that the exercise in the gym would come to my aid. We found our way to the start of the Gorge Brook trail and our day began. From the onset, I knew this hike would be a memorable one. We could hear the wind picking up force and blowing about us, but the ledges seemed to act as a breakfront. We had the benefit of the sound without the cold. It was strange. We climbed along the bank of the Gorge Brook for quite a long time, thanking God that the black flies were not too bad this year. We had picked a prime fly time to be in the woods.

Just as we left the area of the brook, we experienced a light rain which cooled us just enough to make us comfortable. The effort of the climb had started to heat us up. We welcomed the rain but hoped that it would not become too intense or cause the beautiful scenery to be lost in a fog. We were granted our wish. At the point where the trail left the brook, the switchbacks began and hiking became easier. We spent quite a bit of time at the lookout to see Pleides Slide. We worried that we had spent too much time there, but hesitated about leaving. It was as if we were being told by some force to sit back and wait. We were rewarded by the sight of an eagle soaring past on his way to hunt in the mountains. We were glad for the impulse to settle in and wait for Nature to give us this gift. The climb continued. The aroma of the woods was a treat. Each breath brought a myriad of tree and flower essences that warmed the body and the soul. It was as though we were merging into one with the Earth around us. These moments are rare indeed and we took full time to enjoy it all. We soon arrived at the timberline and followed the cairns to the summit of the mountain.

There were a few other couples on the mountain that morning and we all seemed inclined to keep our distance one from the other. It was nice to see others around, but we wanted to be alone, and to talk to others would have been too great an effort. I have never experienced this before or since that day. Mike and I enjoyed our lunch without exchanging a complete sentence. Kristyn had packed lunch for us and we found hard cheese, rolls, fruit and slices of carrots and celery. Boxed juices that had been frozen the night before were also included. They are perfect for climbing because by the time we arrive at the top, they are still ice cold, but no longer slushy—even if they are, they are still very refreshing. Enclosed was a note from Kristyn, who wrote that she hoped that we were having a good time. I lay back after lunch about as contented as I could ever expect to be. It was a perfect day!

After our allotted time had passed, I became aware that Mike was moving about picking up the remains from lunch and packing to get ready to start down the mountain. We promised each other that we would one day return to this mountain to enjoy the views and the companionship that we had shared on this, the first hike of 1991. The hike down was uneventful and the dreaded fog had set in to a degree, hiding the lookouts from us. I enjoy the trips down from any hike more than the ascent. Going uphill, I find that I am always more tired and that I expend much more effort for my lungs and my legs. I need to take frequent breaks just to catch my breath. On the way down, even though my knees take jolts due to the grade of the trail, I feel better all over. Jim Wilton and Nancy Seavey find that the opposite is true for them. They prefer the strain on the lungs and calves to the knee jolts. I guess we are all different. We were sincerely pleased that we had taken our fill of the scenery on the way up. We arrived home in time to take Kristyn with us to Yoken's, a favorite restaurant in Portsmouth, for supper.

MOUNT CABOT

Elevation: 4170
Date: June 2, 1991
Trail: Mount Cabot Trail

CARL AND NANCY SEAVEY called to ask if I would like to join them on this hike. It is the furthest one from where we live so we decided to do it early in the season. It was a most pleasurable ride to the mountain, especially since I did not have to drive. This in itself was unusual since I usually volunteer to drive as a penance to my hiking companions for progressing so slowly. We stopped for breakfast and drove the long road to Jefferson. I was glad that Carl was driving because I am not sure I could have found the area by myself. The Seaveys had already done this trail before on skis, so they knew where the trailhead was. We left our extra clothes and gear in the car, passed under a gate, and started on the trail.

This trail was one of the easiest to follow. There was not a single moment of doubt as to whether or not I was on the wrong path. The blazes on the trail were clear and concise.

I may have mentioned before that Carl and Nancy are very tall and have long legs. We started off at a relatively low elevation area along a road. Less than a hundred yards in, I felt uncomfortably hot and rushed. I could not catch my breath and worried that if I felt this bad this early in the hike, how would I do on the real climb? We plowed on ahead, none of us speaking, each lost in his own world of the hike. Nancy had a problem with her pack and needed to take a break to fix the pack and to peel off a layer of clothes. I took the time to set off by myself. I needed to be alone to set my own pace. I remember mumbling some cadence songs from Army marches to help myself. The squirrels did not appreciate my efforts and the woods became still except for the racing thumps of my heart in my ears. Finally it happened. The pace and cadence lined up and I was able to move less erratically. The Seaveys caught up with me as we arrived at the stream crossing. At that point, I looked at the *AMC Guidebook* and discovered why I had been so breathless. We were half an hour ahead of guidebook time. I felt much better and told the Seaveys that I needed to slow down on the next section of the hike. They agreed to slow down and told me that I should have mentioned it a long time ago. They were right. Nancy told me at the rest stop that she had broken her wrist last winter around this point. We crossed the stream up a way from the trail and found it relatively easy to manage. The climb became more difficult at that point.

We took a lunch break at an old cabin that was in pretty poor shape. I could see that it could be a life-saver in the winter months and thought it too bad that we hikers, the only ones up in the mountains, have not taken responsibility to at least pick up our own trash from the area. We enjoyed the views from the area around the fire tower and after lunch went on to the wooded summit of Mount Cabot. It was a good hike with great companions. Carl began a tradition of exchanging jokes or amusing stories that we used on future hikes to keep up the good moods. It was easy for me to keep pace with the Seaveys on the hike out. We actually enjoyed a conversation all the way down! Carl helped Nancy and I across the stream and we finished the descent.

There was a little country store that we stopped in for cold drinks and to use the potty. We talked with the owner who was remodeling the place around an old-fashioned round wood/coal stove located in the center of the store. The bathroom was to be rebuilt in an old food storage locker. Nancy and I planned to return to do Mount Waumbek later in the season and promised to stop by on the way home. We hoped that he would keep and enhance the old-fashion flavor of the place. It sounded good! I wrapped myself up in Carl's sweatshirt on the drive home and was able to watch the scenery as Nancy drove and Carl slept. We stopped at Carl's favorite spot on the way home. He has a tradition of stopping at Rosie's Restaurant in Tamworth for hot dogs and fries after his hikes. Good tradition!

Hey, Lady!

LIBERTY–FLUME

MOUNT LIBERTY   Elevation: 4459
MOUNT FLUME   Elevation: 4328
Date: June 29, 1991
Trail: Liberty Spring Trail

JIM WILTON wanted to go camping to share the great outdoors with his son. We had already camped out together once before and had had a good time so we added Kristyn to our group and decided to climb the southern peaks on the Franconia Range. We picked a weekend to go and planned the various aspects of the trip in meetings during the winter. Carla underwent several work schedule changes and was going to be unable to spend the night on the mountain. She decided to come along with us and go solo off the mountain after the hike. Since she is a fast hiker and quite experienced, we figured that she would be fine. Kristyn had been on several hikes, but had not done much of a physical nature since her high school graduation a year before. We talked about getting in shape, but she, like many people mistook being of low body fat and weight to be synonymous with being in shape. She borrowed a pair of my hiking boots and planned to wear her old pack. It was a disaster waiting to happen. We were all loaded pretty heavily with tents, packs, cooking gear, and food. We had divided things up pretty fairly. The drive up to the mountains was uneventful. Kristyn slept in the back seat while I talked with Mike to help him stay awake. Carla took her own car, while Jim and Sean rode up in Jim's new Jeep.

We had to park quite a distance from the trailhead and the walk in seemed long. Kristyn had some trouble with her pack and had to spend valuable time with her dad getting it to fit properly. At the onset, we divided into groups. Sean buzzed on ahead with Carla in hot pursuit. His style was to rush on ahead with Carla, wait for us slow folks to catch up, and run off again. We were lucky that Carla, amongst all of us, had the fortitude to keep up with Sean! Kristyn stayed in the rear with Jim who was loaded down with both his and Sean's gear. Mike and I were in the middle. I kept dropping back to be with Kristyn from time to time. It was too bad that she had not broken in the boots to fit her feet. Her payment was in the form of painful hot spots on her heels! Fortunately, Jim was able to give her immediate relief and prevented the blisters that would have been inevitable. I think the most striking memory of the hike up was the color green. The trees were in full bloom and the sun, filtering through the them, gave a green tint to everything around us. It was like looking through a stained glass window. I took a long distance shot of Sean on a rock, and he looked like a leprechaun. Even his skin had a greenish hue. We had chosen to take the Liberty Spring Trail to the tent platforms and go on to the peaks in the afternoon. According to the book, it should have taken only two hours to arrive at that point. Two and a half hours into the hike, we realized that we were going to take a lot longer.

The second half of the trail was upward bound with no relief. Even our breaks were spent on uneven ground and we did not get much of a rest at those times. I began to feel a desperation that I would not get to the camp ground. I tried to phase out and separate myself from the hike, but that did not work. I felt physically ill from the effort of hiking. Each step was a challenge. I found myself praying that Carla would soon shout that she had arrived at the tent platforms. I thought about getting to the ridge to hike in the open and that thought sustained me. We all carried so much weight on our backs. I looked behind me at the others and they were bent over at the middle to compensate for the grade of the trail. It was very difficult. Finally Carla shouted that she had reached the tent sites. We joined her shortly and we decided to have lunch before planning what to do next. We had taken over three hours to do this two hour climb. We set up the three tents and relaxed with our lunch. Refreshed by the break and lunch, we decided to go on with the hike.

We packed an emergency bag to share along with extra water and started up the path cut into the hillside. We arrived at the Franconia Ridge Junction in about fifteen minutes. I just love the word "ridge"! We walked more easily and lighter at this point and the trail flew by beneath our feet. We arrived at the summit of Mount Liberty in no time and assessed our situation. We took a decent break at this point and took several photos from the edge of the mountain. I remember holding on for dear life as Mike positioned himself between me and the rather steep cliff. The photo would be a better one if the look of panic could be airbrushed off my face! Sean did not want to hike any further and Kristyn volunteered to take him back to the campsite. Carla and I left first to start the trail to Mount Flume. For the two of us, there was not a decision to make… we were going on ahead- regardless of what the others wanted to do. We took off at a slow gallop. We arrived in no time at all and stood at the peak waving back at Kristyn and Sean who had agreed to wait to see us arrive at the top. What a great feeling it was to be up at this peak! It was like being at the top of the world. The steep rock slide down the side of the mountain made it seem so isolated from our world. Mike and Jim soon joined us at the top and we took time to snap some photos of each other. I have to say that at that moment I had never felt stronger or more alive in my life. After enjoying the fantastic panorama, Carla and I started to return to Mount Liberty. Jim and Mike were behind us and I expected them to pass us as they always had. I stopped to pick up a weird tiny rock that had the outline of a human skull on it and heard Mike remark to Jim that he had never seen me climbing so well. I was very proud and admitted to myself that it was true. I was very comfortable with the rapid pace that Carla had set. We spent some more time at Mount Liberty and then returned to the campsite. Sean was asleep in his tent and Kristyn was resting in Jim's hammock.

The rest of the afternoon passed quickly. We worried about Carla who had rushed off to get back to her car, but assured ourselves that she would have reached the trailhead in record time if she had kept up the pace she started with. The tent platform was a nice solid place to share a wonderful meal. The manager stopped by to collect our fees and told us where to go to see the sunset. We wandered over past the spring and climbed up onto the structure built for the viewing. We sat close to each other to share our body heat and watch the setting sun. This had a surrealistic aura about it. The sun went down in stages, much like it does on the beach. It was slow and steady. The mountain in front of the sun seemed to absorb the orb into itself and the rays spiraled out around the mountain, blessing it with the last touches of its light. We sat for a while after the sunset passing a flask of Dominican brandy between us. As usual, I had left my flashlight behind at the tent. Obviously I had not associated the word sunset with darkness. Mike and Jim had no trouble navigating in the blackness, but I found myself bumping into everyone and stepping on every root available. I have no night vision. We enjoyed a hot drink and settled down for the night.

I had taken the last of the hot water and filled my canteen to take to bed with me like a hot water bottle. I donned my Barbizon nightgown (flannel on the inside and satin on the outside) and crawled into my down bag. Sleep never comes easy to me even at home, and I tossed around a while before Morpheus, the god of sleep, captured me in his arms. I awakened shaking at about two in the morning. I was disoriented and very cold. Since the last incident on Mount Monroe, I had worried about hypothermia, and there I was, in its grip again. I could not believe it. I also could not move. I lay there shivering and trying to wake Mike to help me. My bag is a down mummy-style and I did not have the hand coordination necessary to get the thing unzipped. I finally managed to bump Mike enough to alert him, and he figured out the problem. By that time I had managed to move the tent across the platform to the edge by shaking so hard, and Mike had to go out and pull us back to a safe spot. He managed to get me something warm to drink and put our bags together. Positioning ourselves in spoon fashion, I was finally able to stop shaking. Mike admitted in the morning that he had contemplated evacuating me off the mountain at one point during the night. The rest of the night passed without incident. I guess I have to really know my tent mates on future hikes!

The day dawned clear and dry, and I had only sore jaws to remind me of the difficulty of the night before. We had fantastic hot coffee and a light breakfast before we had to leave this delightfully maintained site. The hike out was wonderfully all downhill and was accomplished in less than half the time it had taken to ascend. We were all happy about what we had done. At that point, the commitment to finish the forty-eight four thousand mountains was officially made.

SOUTH KINSMAN MOUNTAIN

Elevation: 4358
Date: August 8, 1991
Trails: Lonesome Lake Trail
Fishin' Jimmy Trail
Kinsman Ridge Trail

HAVING MADE the commitment to join the Four Thousand Foot Club, it became evident that it would be necessary to return to this area and climb the mountain that I had left without conquering back in 1985. I would like to say that it was with great enthusiasm that I approached this task, but alas it would not be true. I had two warring sides within myself and they pulled me apart emotionally. My saccharine side told me that Carla would be coming with me and therefore it was sure to be a great climb, that it was August and I could be rewarded by a frosty dip in the lake on the return trip, that it would be a wonderful day and a challenging hike, and that it did not matter that I had not done the hike with Mike. My sour grapes side recounted that I had been too insecure in 1985, I had been stupid, I would be tramping on ground I had already covered once before, and I had, in fact, made a mistake. I could not get into the mood of the hike from the start and I can only pray that Carla did not suffer whenever the sour grapes side kicked in!

We got an early start and feasted on coffee, bagels and cream cheese on the way up to the Lafayette Place Campground. Carla had done this climb the previous Fall and was looking forward to being back in the woods again. She was going full tilt and was finishing her forty-eight mountains. We made it to the lake in very good time and spent a little time looking at the displays around the common room of the Lonesome Lake Hut. I found the log book where Mike and I had written a few lines six years before. We had a hot drink and discussed our plans with one of the Crew from the hut system. We found our way to the base of the Fishin' Jimmy Trail and began our climb.

As usual, the weather was damp, but we were fortunate that it was not cold. We were comfortable in shorts and tee shirts for the climb and we did not need to drag on the rain gear. The gentle and intermittent rain was a blessing because it kept humidity and heat down to a minimum and the bugs stayed away. The only thing to annoy me was the signs of human littering. We are truly nasty beasts. Whenever I had to leave the trail, I found evidence of paper and human waste left out in the open. I am not easily grossed out, but this was bad. Animals do not take waste away nor steal dirty papers. Trash sits there until it rots—usually more than one season. I found that for myself it is convenient to carry two separate small sandwich bags, one for dry tissue and one for soiled. It is easy to toss the bag away at the end of the hike. Ecologists may get a slight shiver at the use of plastic, but I think it is better than polluting the trails and water with all of our waste paper. As for solid waste, it only takes a couple of minutes and very little effort to dig a small trench a few inches deep and bury it.

Carla kept me laughing about her previous adventures on this hike when one of the hikers, who happened to be male, turned out to be somewhat eccentric. In the morning they found him naked as a Jaybird taking deep Yoga-type breaths on the porch. I was sorry to have missed that particular hike. We worked our way up to the top of North Kinsman.

I was on new ground and was able to shake away the sour grapes part of my mentality. We did not take a very long break at the top, but marched on to find the summit of South Kinsman. The trail between the two summits is rather rough terrain and involves a bit of stretching to breach the areas between footsteps. I found myself sitting down quite a few times to avoid over extending myself and risk falling. Carla and I exchanged stories about work and hikes, and the time went by quickly. We had some difficulty finding the actual top of South Kinsman and were fortunate to be helped by a Crew member out for a stroll in the mountains on his day off. He showed us where the peak was. We reached the top and found a nice flat area to relax, enjoy the scenery, and eat lunch. The rain had stopped and the views were fantastic. The leaves had already started to turn red in some of the areas in the distance and they blended so beautifully with the blue of the sky and the dark green background. The clouds seemed too perfect to be real. Mother Nature was smiling on us. We took the time to be duly thankful to her!

We checked our watches and decided that we had to get moving if we were to return in good time. Carla set a moderate pace to lead us back on the same trail to the hut. Carla had become quite a hiker and I sensed that she could teach me a lot about the sport—if I could keep up with her! I was able to take a quick dip in Lonesome Lake with a few brave souls crazy enough to test the strength of their lungs and hearts against this frigid water. We were late getting out of the woods, although the going was not that rough. We did not get to the car until after five o'clock. We got supper on the road and enjoyed the remainder of our time together on the drive home. It was a good hike.

MOUNT WAUMBEK

Elevation: 4005
Date: September 5, 1991
Trail: Starr King Trail

NANCY HAD an unexpected day off and called me to see if I could take the time off to go climb Mount Waumbek. The hospital census was low and my nursing unit was agreeable to my taking a day off. Our husbands would be unable to join us. It was decided to leave early the next day to take our trip. I remembered with pleasure the last hike in that vicinity, namely, Mount Cabot. I hoped that the trail would be as easy to follow as the previous one. The weather on the Seacoast was rainy, but the report for the mountain region was all right, and we decided to take a chance and trust the weatherman! We had breakfast at Jeanine's Bakery and drove the long road up to the base of the trail. Fortunately, Nancy has a good memory and sense of direction, because I have neither.

We sorted out our gear. Weather changes fast in this area and we had packed accordingly. The *AMC Guidebook* had listed the approximate time to be three hours to the summit, so we thought it necessary to pack emergency clothes and gear. The weather at the trailhead was quite mild for September, but we could not count on that to continue. After half an hour of sorting things out, we began the hike.

My wishes were partially granted, as the trail was laid out very well with a gradual ascent, not easy, but not extremely difficult. Nancy and I were able to keep up a flow of conversation for most of the hike. This is a good sign for me, because if a trail has too much of a grade, my lungs can only suck in enough air to breath, and talking is not possible. Nancy was able to saunter along beside me and she took frequent breaks to admire the sights of Nature along the trail while I plodded along. We were glad to have left the rain behind us and we were thoroughly enjoying the hike. We took a very short break at the summit of Starr King and went on to the wooded summit of Mount Waumbek. We took photographs at the top for my album, and we returned to a wonderful spot to enjoy our lunch on the hot granite rocks overlooking the wilderness and the highway far below us.

Nancy and I, though we have a great time together, are total opposites in many ways. She is very tall, slender, and dark, while I am only 5'4", not slender, and fair. Nancy is always cold, and I am generally hot. We have been hiking together for so long that we do not notice the differences anymore. We just do our own thing and we do not hesitate to ask each other to

change something if one's behavior impinges on the comfort of the other. For example, I ask Nancy to slow down or to take breaks much more frequently than she would need to, and Nancy sometimes asks me to keep moving if she gets too cold. We try to honor each others' needs. At our lunch, we were amused by the observations of a third party. When we arrived at a good vantage point, I took off my shoes and socks, and was enjoying the breeze on my bare legs and arms. Nancy, on the other hand, put on wind pants, her Polar fleece shirt, wind breaker, woolen hat with the ear flaps down, and mittens. We sat on the rocks enjoying ourselves without paying much attention to the incongruous sight we made. A couple vacationing from Britain came upon us, and stared at us, perplexed. They finally asked us if we intended to end up at the same location. I suppose it did look as if one of us was Alaska-bound while the other was headed for Hawaii! We all enjoyed a laugh at their observation.

After lunch, we found that we had plenty of time to explore the area, and found the site of an old house, including an old granite fireplace. The building had obviously burned down many years ago. We sat on the rocks envying the people who had lived there, for it had a wonderful view all around it. The clouds overhead were perfect. They were the large fluffy kind of clouds that break up like cotton candy into various shapes and figures. We took some time to enjoy imagining various mythical and animal creatures in the sky before we decided to come back to earth... and the car. Our descent was slow and casual. Nancy had had a bad experience on a previous climb when the beating of her toes against the fronts of her boots had blackened her toenails. She was making an effort to descend at a slower, gentler pace and I found that much to my liking. We arrived at the car none the worse for wear, and not very tired. We stopped by the little country store to find the work not finished, but progressing well. We did not stay too long, but we bought some snacks to munch on the way home. We felt very lucky because it was still raining when we reached the coast. Mike had been so positive that we would arrive home cold and wet, that he had made a wonderful supper for me. I felt doubly blessed!

THE BONDS

MOUNT BONDCLIFF Elevation: **4265**
MOUNT BOND Elevation: **4698**
WEST BOND Elevation: **4540**
OWL'S HEAD Elevation: **4025**
Date: **September 13-14, 1991**
Trails: **Wilderness Trail**
Bondcliff Trail
Franconia Brook Trail

IT WAS the best of plans, it was the worst of plans! I spent part of my vacation working out the details of this hike. Most of the participants saw and evaluated the plans, but though many said it would be long, no one suggested that it was stupid or physically impossible. Like lambs to the slaughter, we packed up the cars and drove to the Wilderness Trail off the Kancamagus Highway. Mike was up to such a hike, and I had never felt stronger. Carl and Nancy were ready as they had spent some time recently at Mount Katahdin in Maine, and their daughter, Bonnie, was a very physical young woman who had her parents' great legs and endurance—assets to any climb. Carla, of course, was in wonderful shape for the climb and was anxious to get hiking this Fall. Dr. Janet Howe, as a young girl of ten or so, had helped her father place some of the benchmarks in the White Mountains and was anxious to see where some of them were, and how they had withstood the years in the mountains. Jim and Sean were ready so the only unknown factor was Sean's buddy, Stephen. We predicted that the two boys would bounce like gazelles along the trail with no problems. It was exciting as we stood together at the parking lot and took a group photo showing a healthy group with great anticipation of fun reflected in all the faces!

The Wilderness Trail is a wonderful walk. It is a shaded area that is, in actuality, an old railroad bed. Along the way, there are many railroad ties, spikes and some old coal. It is very flat, and the only challenge is to stay alert enough so that you do not become mesmerized and trip over a raised tie or spike. Nancy managed to do just that and was our first casualty of the day. She was fortunate to only get a bump on her forehead and had to put up with the bump as well as our chuckles. We were able to get going at a very rapid rate, and soon found ourselves in two distinct groups. The Seaveys and Frachers with Carla ahead, and the Wilton group and Janet behind. Jim was overburdened with gear. He was physically bent over as he carried a tent to sleep the four of them, all of his own gear, all of the boys stuff, and all of their food. The pack was a wonder to behold. I would not hazard a guess as to how much weight he was bearing. He said he could manage it, though he would be moving much slower than we were. Janet decided to stay with Jim and the boys. By the time we reached the Camp 16 site, we had already walked about five miles. I was tired and the weight of the pack was getting to me. On the positive side, I had purchased a new pair of boots for this hike called Hi Techs, and they were wonderful. They gave the impression of walking on clouds... very soft with good support. The only problem was that they were spruce green and purple. Carl kept making remarks about the boots and we all laughed at his comments. We arrived at the trail junction in just under two hours—which was excellent time!

We were all in great spirits at this time and continued along the Bondcliff Trail. The grade was just slightly greater, so it was still a relatively easy time hiking. The only major problem we had was when we mistook a well-used camping site footpath for the real trail and followed it across the stream. We found no markers or blazes to guide us further. It was necessary for half the group to stay on one side of the brook and the rest had to return to the other side and fan out to find a trail marker. We had crossed the brook mistakenly and had lost some time finding our way. It did not really upset anyone, but we took time to write a note for Jim and Janet to keep them from making the same mistake. While searching for a proper campsite, we stumbled onto a well-used area. There was adequate space for the four tents, and an established fire ring with all the stones in place. We discussed its only failing, which was that it was really too close to the stream. We rationalized that we would do better to use this established area, rather than to intrude further on Nature and tramp down new vegetation in order to settle down in a new site. We set up the tents and put our campsite in order. The wood was set by the stones for the campfire that night, and all was ready by the time lunch was served. We sat in comfort to eat. Jim and the group joined us when we were getting ready for the next part of the climb. Jim's party decided that they had had enough walking for one day and

Hey, Lady!

would stay at the campsite to play and to do Bondcliff the next day. They would come back to the same site the next night. Smart move!

After crossing a relatively dry stream-bed, the true climbing began. We were basically light packing by now with water and snacks the high priority items for us all. With a little boost from Mike and Carl, we were all able to scramble up the last challenging cliff to the top of Bondcliff. I am glad that we had not heard much about ticks in New Hampshire as yet, because I am sure this part of the trail would have had me totally neurotic. The trail is very narrow and the branches brush against you the entire way!

The views from Bondcliff are astounding. There are no signs of civilization. All one can see are the mountains and the sky. We took many photographs from all the vantage points. I would take one picture, move two feet and be sure that this view was so different that it, too, needed to be documented! We were having such a great time that we could have been contented to just go this far. In fact, Mike and Nancy decided to do just that. They decided to stay a while at the top and retire to the campsite for the remainder of the afternoon. The rest of us moved on. Carl Seavey had completed all of the four-thousand footers except for West Bond, and that was one of the goals that had been set. I hope he does not mind my recounting how this had happened. A couple years of before, he and Nancy had gone hiking/camping with a group and had done most of the mountains in the area. They set up tents at the Mount Goyette area and bedded down. Sleep came hard for Carl and when the group tried to get him to wake up early to climb to the summit of West Bond to watch the sunrise, he rolled over and went back to sleep. He had no plans to finish all the forty-eight mountains at that time. Now here he was, back to climb West Bond. We moved on along the trail to Mount Bond, looking back at Mike and Nancy, who were sitting on a huge rock, enjoying the sun!

In a little less than two hours we reached the second summit. We took a short break at this point and ate some of the trail foods that we had carried along. We took additional pictures although the sights were not quite as dramatic as those we had just experienced on Bond Cliff. I was very tired. I looked back towards Bondcliff to see if Mike was still at the peak. I saw a man with a sparkling white tee shirt come out on a rock outcropping, take a single step in our direction, and start to wave. I took off my bandanna and slowly waved back. I told Carla, who was standing beside me, to wave to Mike. She saw him and complied. I swear to you that we had passed no one on the trail since the Wilderness area at seven in the morning, and that no one had passed us, or Mike and Nancy. When I told Mike much later that night in the tent about how I had felt encouraged by his waving to me to go on, he informed me that he and Nancy had not waited for us to get to the summit, but had gone down the mountain. There had been nobody left at the Bondcliff summit. No one to wave at us. The hairs stood up on the back of my neck. I did not tell anyone about it, and neither did Mike.

I looked at my watch and felt a shiver of nervousness because the hour was late and we still had not reached West Bond. Carl and Bonnie decided to backtrack. I just could not do it. I had already been in the trap of walking all day only to turn back before finishing my planned hike at the Kinsmans. I would have climbed the rest of the way on my knees to avoid doing that to myself again. Besides, the book stated that West Bond was a mere twenty minutes away. I would not turn back and Carla supported my decision. I felt responsible for Carl not finishing his last hike as I climb so much slower than the rest. Carla and I left the Seaveys and started as fast as we could towards the last peak. We were swiftly passed by the Seaveys. Carl was mumbling something about stupidity under his breath as he passed us. I felt better knowing that he would finish as planned. I left my pack in the col, or hollow, just previous to the final ascent, (probably in hopes that someone would steal it and I would not have to carry it anymore), and went on lighter in step. We all arrived at the top in considerably more time than twenty minutes. Carl popped the cork on the traditional bottle of champagne that Bonnie had carried and we all watched as the liquid shot up into the sky. It must have been the jostling motion combined with the heat and the altitude! We all took a symbolic sip, took a couple of pictures to commemorate the occasion, and got ready to start back. It was after seven o'clock!

Water was pretty low by then, so we filled the emptiest canteens with the warm champagne and started back down the trail. I felt very uneasy about the climb back. By the time we arrived at Mount Bond, the evening shadows were evident and it was pretty clear that we would have to hike at least part of the way in the dark. I just prayed that we would be past Bondcliff before the sun set completely! The pressure of rushing made my footsteps very unsure and I found myself completely drained of energy. I wanted to cry and probably would have if there had been the time or any tears in me. The trail was hard and uneven beneath my feet and I felt guilty. I judged myself severely in that it had been my decision to plan this hike, and my decision to go on when the others had voted to turn back. If anything happened to any of us, the responsibility would be no one's but mine! I craved water, but the water was all gone. I do not particularly like the taste of champagne, and warm champagne is even worse. We sipped it sparingly. By the time we arrived at the summit of Bondcliff, we had given up even the pretense of trying to talk to each other. It was too much effort. We were exhausted. Carla, bless her heart, fumbled in her pack and was able to come up with two squashed plums that we divided amongst ourselves, relishing the sweet nectar and juice. Just as darkness began its' reign for the night, Carl helped each one of us down over the last cliff. We had made it down Bondcliff safely. Each of us had had the foresight to pack head lamps and we donned them quickly. Nancy had provided extra flashlights when the group split and we put them to good use. We walked slowly, both from the bone-wrenching fatigue and the danger of falling in the dark. I plodded on along behind Carla who followed Bonnie. Carl brought up the rear, still occasionally mentioning how stupid we were! It was put one foot ahead of the other, steady myself, change weight, and repeat, until there was nothing else left in my brain to even think about. Step, step, step. The darkness was enhanced by the claustrophobic press of the vegetation all the way down. The branches hitting off the person in front would often sneak past their tired restraining hand to hit the person behind. The stinging hits were ignored, or not even felt. We just concentrated on getting down and not falling. Finally we arrived at the stream bed and turned on the road to begin our final hike to the campsite.

We arrived at the campfire at ten o'clock. I sat down on a log, too tired to even speak. Janet remarked later that some of the patients in her psychiatric practice looked better than we did. I did not have the strength to lift a cup of water to my lips so Mike had to help. I do not remember any noise. I saw Jim using the water filter, and saw Sean and Stephen come out of the tent. They had waited up for us, but had given up and gone to bed. They came out, took one look at us, and went back into the tent. There must have been voices or other noises, perhaps the snapping of logs in the fire at least, but I cannot remember any of it. The others were being attended to by those who had not done the marathon. We were all fed hot suppers and helped into sleeping bags for the night. I talked to Mike for about three minutes and fell into an exhausted and dreamless sleep. I awakened in just about the same position I had fallen asleep. Believe it or not, I felt great! I had been certain that I would be terribly stiff and sore from the hike but felt no pain at all. I do not think I would ever want to walk in the dark again, but I would like to go back to Bondcliff and camp out!

The next morning we were greeted by Sean and Stephen with reports of how horrible we had looked and acted the night before. Personally, I was just grateful that we had not been hurt during the hike. After breakfast, we separated into two groups again. Jim's party planned to climb Bondcliff this morning, and the rest of us would backtrack to the Lincoln Brook Trail and the base of Owl's Head with the plan to climb to its' summit the next morning. We pushed onward, taking our first break at the old Camp 16 site where we had a fruit snack and discussed the hike we had done the day before. It was at this point that I learned that no one had actually believed that we would be able to accomplish the feat of the three mountains in one day. Fine time to tell me about it! The walk to the Franconia Brook Trail was quite pleasant. We walked along and teased each other about how we walked, talked, thought, worked, and any other thing we knew about each other. Carl began harassing me again about my ugly boots which had remained miraculously clean. It was all in good fun and the time passed quickly. When we arrived at the junction of Franconia Brook Trail and Lincoln Brook Trail, we were all ready for a food break. We opted to have an early lunch. We relaxed and removed our packs. We had started packing teriyaki strips on an earlier hike and now shared them to everyone's pleasure. Peanut butter and jelly sandwiches on Syrian bread and fruit finished the menu. I was starting to feel tired, probably because of yesterday's hike. As we sat by the railroad tracks I gazed longingly at the flat area we would take to go home. It was not easy to turn away from the tracks and begin the ascent up the Lincoln Brook Trail.

The three Seaveys set out at a rapid pace, leaving Mike and me struggling along behind with Carla. Carla was able to set a much better pace for me to follow and we went about the phasing-out process of a hike when one is too tired to think about what one is doing. We plodded along putting one foot in front of the other and moving ever onwards and upwards. Mike could not believe Carla's stamina. She was never the one to call a break, no matter how long we traveled. I would vow that it would not be me to ask for the next stop if it killed me, but most of the time, it would be. Thank God Mike's boots became untied once in a while, or it would have always been me! I think that this trail would have seemed better if I were not already tired. The trail follows the Franconia Brook most of the way with several easy crossings. We were twice rerouted due to washouts on the trail, but all in all there were no major problems. The grade is constant which made it a difficult climb for me. I like the breaks in pitch to help relax my legs and lungs! We had lost sight of the Seavey's after about ten minutes of climbing and we were not to see them again until we reached the base of Owl's Head. We were lucky that Carla had done this hike before because we were confused at the end of the trail. She kept us on the straight and narrow. We finally heard voices and found the Seaveys relaxing by the brook at the campsite. They had arrived quite a bit before us. It was only a little after three in the afternoon at this point, and I thought I would like to go on to the summit then, rather than wait until morning. Mike declined, saying that he did not want to do it now, or in the morning, or perhaps ever. Bonnie was not interested. Carl and Nancy also declined. Carl absolutely hates this mountain because he had a bad experience the last time he climbed it. Apparently there was a thunderstorm and the lightning was all around them as they were rushing to get back to the base. The rocks on the slide were hazardous and at least three people were hurt by falling stones and small rock slides during their descent. As if that were not bad enough, Carl lost his boots to the sucking mud in the brook on the trail out. He did not have a single fond memory of this area. As I stood there deliberating my dilemma, Carla handed me my pack, and put hers on. She would go with me. I could have hugged her. Carla had said earlier that she did not want to repeat Owl's Head either, since she had shared Carl's experience. She is a true friend. We went to the base of the slide trail where a single glove on a stick pointed to the trail to take. I had never climbed on a slide before. I had to place my feet as firmly as possible and not linger. If I did, I would feel the rock layers shift slightly and I would slide back a few feet with each step upwards. Carla was good at it, and by following her example, I was able to make progress up the slope. To be frank, I rather enjoyed it.

We soon arrived at the top of the slide where the trail goes into the woods. It was getting rather late, and Carla was not completely sure about which way to go. She went on ahead, leaving me further and further behind. I looked up and she was about fifty yards ahead, then a hundred, then she disappeared from my view. I was uneasy. I knew she was scouting the way for us, but I became apprehensive and struggled to find which way she had gone. There was a small, narrow, and slightly overgrown path off to my right, and I thought for a second that I saw Carla's red pack in the distance, so I walked off that way. I called out her name once in a while, not too loudly, for I did not want to hear the fear in my voice. She did not respond. After a short time, I felt a sharp tug on my backpack and thought for a split second that Mike had changed his mind and had followed us up after all. I turned around happily to see him, but no one was there. I looked around to find a low hanging branch to explain what had grabbed the pack, but there was none. There was no logical explanation. For the second time in two days, the hackles rose on the back of my neck. Carla came flying down the trail at the same time and just about knocked me over in her haste. She reported that as she walked, she looked down to see if the trail she was following was the right one. When she did, she caught a reflection of a man in a white tee shirt in her glasses. She said that he was slowly turning his head from side to side as if to answer her question about the trail. When she turned to face him, the trail was empty. Needless to say, she beat a hasty retreat. She asked me if the man on Bondcliff yesterday had been Mike, and I admitted that it had not been him. As we talked together about the incident, we both glanced down to find a cairn marking the trail sitting less than a foot away from us. We scurried to the top of the mountain, and turned back to get back down the trail before it got dark. We were not too anxious to be alone up there anymore.

We were rewarded for our efforts by beautiful sunset views of the Franconia Ridge west of Owl's Head. The walking was a bit shaky, and our ankles were sore from the constant pounding and bracing necessary to avoid a fall, but I cannot say that it was unpleasant. In a remarkably short time, we saw a tent site to our right and were astounded to find that we were down

Hey, Lady!

the slide already. In our absence, the gang had set up all the tents and prepared our supper for us. Around the campfire that night, we related our stories about the mysterious man in the white tee shirt. I wonder if anyone else has seen this man or knows who he could be.

In retrospect, I do not think that this peak is as terrible as some people say. The views coming down made it worth the trip. The hike in is certainly long, and I would suggest that a good look at a reliable weather forecast is in order. One should plan on hiking in and camping out either before or after the ascent. I would not have wanted to miss this one! The campsite is right beside the river. There are two good sites to choose from. All night long, we were lulled by the sound of the river flowing swiftly by us.

The next day dawned somewhat cloudy and we lost no time having breakfast and packing the gear. The trail down was relatively easy, although muddy. Much to Carl's disgust, my loud-colored boots seemed to repel the mud and shined brightly in purple and green in spite of the way I abused them in the muck. We arrived at the Wilderness Trail in good time and began the flat part of the hike out. With the group's indulgence, I was able to take a good plunge in the Franconia Brook by the bridge, and felt rejuvenated for the remainder of the walk out. A gentle rain started as we walked along the railway, but for the most part we ignored it. Mike was able to try out his new rain hat, and he wore it quite jauntily as we held hands and walked happily all the way to the car. Jim's car was still in the parking lot when we got out, and we hoped that he was all right. We left a note for them, and drove to a local burger place to eat and to decide what to do about the other half of our party. As we sat there, we saw them go by in their car. Later, they told us that they had decided to stop at a children's specialty place for some golf, and then spent some time at the Scottish Celebration, an annual event in Lincoln. It was a good weekend!

A few days later, I developed a problem with my left leg. It became extremely swollen after work that Monday, and I lost the pulse in the foot during the night. The swelling and discoloration lasted for a time, but the intense pain remained constant. I was told by my doctors that I was forbidden to hike any more, and that if I did, they might have to amputate my leg. I was totally devastated by this news and went in search of a doctor who could give me a definitive diagnosis and cure for whatever was wrong with me. I could not find anyone either then, or now. I huddled down for the winter with a heart much colder than the season.

Hey, Lady!

MOUNT
PASSACONAWAY

Elevation: 4060
Date: June 13, 1992
Trail: Dicey's Mill Trail

THIS WAS probably the worst winter of my life. I spent most of it in pain and in search of an answer. I went from cardiologists to general practitioners, neurologists, and even psychics, trying to find a treatment. In time, I figured I would have to learn to live with it. I did take some time off from work and dancing to rest the leg muscles, but that did not make any difference, so I gave up my winter sports and decided to wait until spring when I would think about hiking again. Winter passed without any changes in my leg and I began to get the urge to hit the trail again. One Monday morning, I was discussing my plans for a hike the following weekend in the operating room with Dr. Yeganeh and Dr. Wilton. My orthopedic surgeon, Dr. King, came along and listened for a while. Finally he told me that he had been serious last winter, and that if I climbed again, he might need to do surgery. I will never forget the response that my two friends gave. They asked Dr. King what they would have to do to save my leg in the woods. They agreed to hike with me to finish the four thousand footers. It was clear to them that it was a goal that I had to accomplish and they would do what they could to help me. I have never been so touched by such loyalty, but worried about my decision to lay that type of responsibility on someone else. I cancelled my hike while waiting to hear from a doctor in Boston, and my own physician who was going to consult again with Dr. King and review the reams of reports sent in by the specialists consulted during this time. The different diagnoses contradicted each other. The Boston doctor thought that since all the results were inconclusive, he would say to go on with the hiking. Dr. Pinkerton, weighing all the information, advised against hiking. Nothing was definitive. All was inconclusive.

During this time, my nursing unit was planning a photo exhibit of the staff and took the photograph that made the decision for me. The picture shows me standing against a wall with a transparent mountain range, resembling the Lincoln Lafayette range, superimposed across my heart. Some people would say that the film or the camera was faulty, but in my heart I knew what the picture was saying. As soon as I saw it I knew I that I would have to go hiking.

In the end, it was Mike who joined me on this hike. We packed some extra medical equipment just in case. Mike had done some emergency surgery as a medic in Vietnam, and probably could do the necessary procedure if anything happened on the trail. I chose to do Mount Passaconaway because the trail description seemed easiest of my eight remaining mountains. Carl Seavey had told us that this mountain was a lot of work for little reward and he was to be proven correct. I wanted to get it over with. We arrived in the parking area quite early in the morning and signed the roster in the kiosk there. We then left Ferncroft Road to go through the fence and started up the Dicey's Mill trail. By the time we crossed the Wonalancet Brook, I was covered with perspiration and panting with effort. My mouth felt like it had twenty pounds of cotton in it. I had not slept well for a couple of nights. Alternating joy and apprehension about the hike kept me awake. Mike watched me silently. He was waiting for me to decide for myself whether or not to go on with the hike. I could not express myself and tried to still my pounding heart and swallow the sick feeling in the pit of my stomach so I could go on. I had to get into my mountains again. I had to! With my left leg dragging somewhat behind, we plodded on ahead. I could not make conversation, because I was focused completely inward. Mike was lost in his own thoughts. He was apprehensive about the situation, but he loved me so much that he had chosen to respect my decision and help me with this overwhelming need to accomplish my goal. He carried the pack for most of the time, surrendering it to me only when I asked for it. It was important to me that I carry my own weight on this trip and I wanted to do my share. The trail to the summit of Mount Passaconaway is long and steep. I do not recall any switchbacks or flat areas on which to recover my breath. It went up unrelentingly to the top. We obtained water at the spring at Camp Rich where we met a man who had been camped there for the night. I envied him although I would never dare to stay all alone in such an isolated area! According to the *AMC Guidebook*, we were close to the summit at this time, and I finally got my second wind. We made it to the top in a very short time.

I cannot describe the emotions that overcame me when we arrived at the top. I reached out to Mike in a state of emotional exhaustion and clung to him in a hug that probably lasted fifteen minutes. I do not think I could have stood on my own at that point. We sat down on some rocks for a while and then removed the pack and started looking for the true summit, following the instructions in the Guidebook. It is not always easy to find the unmarked peaks up here, so we scurried about hitting all the high points at the top. I finally climbed a small tree at the Lookout and Mike caught the moment on film.

We and the bugs shared a lunch at the rocks. We feasted on fruit, peanut butter and cheese, and the bugs feasted on us. None of the repellents were working against this group of hungry insects and they buzzed about us trying to get in our nostrils and mouths as we ate. The menthol cough drops worked to keep them out of my face, but tainted the taste of the food. We did not linger any longer than necessary. Carl was right, little reward for all the effort. We hiked down with no problem. My leg felt bad, but it had been worse at times during the winter. I felt lighter in heart than I had in many months. I resolved to finish the hikes as soon as I could safely do so.

Mike and I were both emotionally drained by this hike. I felt badly placing such responsibility on him. I did not realize how drained he was until he almost drove off the road on the way home. I relieved him at the wheel and he fell asleep within minutes and slept all the way home. I said it at the time and still mean it with all my heart. Mike, thank you and I love you!

Hey, Lady!

MOUNT WHITEFACE

Elevation: 4010
Date: June 24, 1992
Trail: Blueberry Ledge Trail

CARLA CAME into the Short Stay Unit to ask if I would like to go on a hike. Nancy had told her about the bad news regarding my leg, but Carla did not say much about it. She only offered to accompany me if I chose to go on with my plans to finish the "4,000 footers." I called her about doing Mount Whiteface a few days later and the date was set. When I told Carla about the doctor's different diagnoses, she agreed to come anyway with the understanding that if I felt anything go wrong, I would turn back right away. We agreed not to mention my leg again.

Carla and I got a very early start. She works days and is used to rising at about five in the morning. We left by six and had a quick breakfast on the way to the highway. I had a cloud of apprehension all around me, but tried to keep it at bay by laughing and joking about anything and everything around us. It was a little phoney, but it worked. By the time we arrived at Ferncroft Road, I had put the fears about my leg on hold and was anxious to get hiking. We parked the car and changed into shorts for the day. We doused ourselves liberally with the bath oil repellent and signed in the register. It was strange to see Mike's and my names from the last hike still on the page! As we were beginning to walk towards the trail, we spotted a strangely- colored bird with a beautiful song. Carla was taking a course in bird watching at UNH and told me that it was a Meadowlark. It seemed like a good omen to see and to hear such a pretty bird at the start of the trail. Carla had selected the trail to take because she had hiked it once before, and judged it to be not too difficult. I was glad Carla knew the way, because the Guidebook uses references such as "take a turn at the first private home" to help you find the trailhead. When I am alone, I question whether someone may have added a house since the last publication and wish they would just put up a small sign with directions on it to guide us!

The trail was a bit steep in places, but with Carla along to talk to, the time passed quickly. We soon found ourselves at a level area with many nice outlooks of the surrounding area. We took a significant break at this point and enjoyed the view. I thanked God for allowing me another hike and thanked Carla for helping me. She never rushed me the entire day, but let me set a rather slow and erratic pace. We had a difficult time on the ledges because some of the wooden braces that are supposed to be secured into the rockface were missing. Carla sort

Hey, Lady!

of scurried up part way, I handed her both packs and slithered up myself and we repeated the process until we arrived at the top. I looked back and did not relish the thought of coming down the same way. We were soon being sprinkled by a light rain and we ran about on the top searching for some sign that we were at the true summit. The wind was picking up, and after about ten minutes of hiking about two hundred yards in every imaginable direction, the rain was not quite so light anymore. We agreed that we must have hit the top and started back down. We did not bother to take a break at that point because we were getting chilled and knew that the longer we waited, the wetter and more treacherous the ledges would become.

We sat down on our backsides and slid one at a time from support to support on the ledges. It scraped our bottoms and messed up our shorts, but we felt safer sitting down for this part of the hike. We took a much shorter time descending that area than ascending. It was not really bad and I rather enjoyed the sliding part. Carla was setting a very good pace at that point, and by arranging my limp I was able to get a good rhythm going that did not hurt my leg. We should have stopped to put on our rain gear, but we decided not to do so because of the good pace we were setting. We did not want to lose it. Instead, I nearly ruined my camera and soaked my entire pack. Carla had wrapped plastic around her fanny pack to keep her camera dry, but even that did not completely protect it. The rain was a driving force. I vowed later to put on rain gear whenever it rained hard on a hike. Getting that wet is not worth the sore throat and the colds we got, to say nothing of the wear and tear on the equipment. We arrived very quickly at the base and followed the signs back to Ferncroft Road. Thanks to Nancy's good advice, we had dry clothes and towels at the car and gratefully dried off and put on clean outfits. We were drenched and cold. With the heater running on full blast, we drove to the Barbecue Pit to fill up on food and hot coffee.

After eating and warming our hands on the coffee cups, we went back to the car to begin the drive back home. Carla asked me to call her about future hikes as she would enjoy repeating any of the ones remaining for me. I thanked her for help and her understanding and promised to call. As we drove home, I was filled with a feeling of accomplishment and well-being. I would be all right!

Hey, Lady!

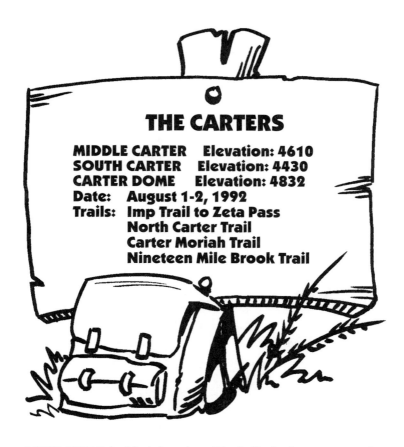

THE CARTERS

MIDDLE CARTER   Elevation: 4610
SOUTH CARTER   Elevation: 4430
CARTER DOME   Elevation: 4832
Date: August 1-2, 1992
Trails: Imp Trail to Zeta Pass
       North Carter Trail
       Carter Moriah Trail
       Nineteen Mile Brook Trail

MIKE AND I decided that since I had climbed two mountains and still had both legs securely, if painfully attached, we might as well keep hiking. We brought the hiking books with us on vacation and decided to camp out along the trail. We invited Nancy and Carl to join us. They agreed and suggested that Carol Pearson, who worked in the operating room, might be interested in coming along. Carol Adams, one of the therapists from the Jackson Gray Building, wanted to come too, so we had a decent size group to keep us company. We held one planning meeting and things were set. We decided to caravan with three cars: one would be left at the Nineteen Mile Brook Trail and the other two at the base of the Imp Trail. We stopped for a quick breakfast on Route 16 and arrived at the trailhead very early. We had no trouble finding a place to park the two cars because no one else was in the area. The Seaveys had climbed the Imp Trail many times and were looking forward to the day, although Nancy was not feeling too well. Carl was the only one who knew she was not up to snuff. She did look a bit pale, but said she was okay to climb. We put on our rather large packs containing our tents, gear, food, and cooking supplies and got underway.

The trail was a pleasant one to start the day on. It did not have much vertical rise, so I did not get overly short of breath, and my legs felt pretty good. The weight of the pack was unusual, so that did make the going a bit slower than it normally would be. We were lucky to find the stream crossing an easy one and continued along, involved in conversation, all the way to the junction of the North Carter Trail. I had planned to take about half an hour longer to reach this part of the trail and was pleased that we were ahead of schedule. We had decided not to go to the summit of North Carter on this trip because of the distance we needed to travel, and I did not want to add any more peaks at this time. I figured that I was pushing my luck to be out here in the first place. We did, however, go to the summit of Mount Lethe since we were so close to it. When we came down, we found Carl and Nancy sitting and talking quite seriously together. They stopped talking when we approached them. I had been so proud of myself for being ahead of Nancy for the first time that I had not questioned why that was possible. Her face was flushed, but she said she was fine. We started to hike again

Hey, Lady!

along the Carter Moriah Trail with Carl and Nancy bringing up the rear. We crested Middle Carter about noon and took a nice leisurely lunch break. Nancy seemed better at this point and we all sat about resting and having an enjoyable meal.

We went along the ridge for a while and then found ourselves in a wooded area without many views. We took pictures at all the sign posts and enjoyed a quick stop at the summit of South Carter. When Nancy and Carl caught up with us, Nancy was in trouble. She was pale, sweaty, and cold. It was plain to see that she was having trouble walking. We had a quick discussion to decide the best thing to do. It was obvious that Nancy would either have to get out of the woods, or we would have to break early and set up an emergency camp to get her off her feet, into dry clothes, and warm. According to the map, the nearest water supply would be at Zeta Pass and we decided to shoot for that area. Normally we would not have camped in that type of area because it does not comply with the guidelines set in the *AMC guidebook*. It was too close to the trail and a water supply, but this was an emergency. We found a relatively flat spot, set up the tents, and got the camp stoves working on boiling water for hot fluids. We were lucky to get settled before the rain and wind started. We were soaked to the skin before we had pumped enough water from the poor excuse for a stream at the bottom of the hill. We were trying out a new filter called the First Need, and found that it worked well, although it was slow. Nancy was settled in her sleeping bag in her Polarfleece and seemed comfortable if she did not have to move around. We ate supper in our tents, and gave up fighting the wind and fog and went to bed at about six thirty that night. I prayed that we had made the right decision and that Nancy would be better in the morning. I worried about my own history of hypothermia, and tried Dr. Pinkerton's advice of stripping down to a chilly tee shirt. It was very cold to start with, but I managed to warm up quickly and was able to fall asleep comfortably.

We awoke at six in the morning and found the weather warming up. There was little fog left and the sun was shining. Nancy was already up drinking coffee. We were all relieved that she was better. She said that she had passed a good night, and she did look more like her normal self. Breakfast was a fast affair and we set about putting the campsite in order. We brought back any brush that we had moved and sticks we had tossed aside. We left no sign that we had been there—which is how it should be! When we were satisfied that we had done all that we could for the site, we put on our packs and went along the trail again. Arriving all too soon at the base of Mount Hight, we decided to climb over it rather than go around it. Someone reasoned that if we did that climb while we were fresh, the path to Carter Dome would not seem so steep. I am not too sure who came up with that theory, but I know God will exact revenge for us! We may have been fresh, but the climb up Mount Hight was hard, especially with the packs that we were carrying. The only saving grace was that the views from the top were fantastic. We sat there watching the puffy clouds float by overhead. We were all back into shorts and tee shirts by then and we hung around at the top since we had all the time in the world to reach the top of Carter Dome. When we had passed sufficient time at the summit, we began to load our packs. Nancy and Carl decided to go back down the Carter Dome Trail and wait for us at the highway. The rest of us pushed on to Carter Dome.

When we arrived at the top of Carter Dome, I had no recollection of having been there before. The last time, the whole area had been in a blanket of fog. This time, there were views all around. We kept our boots on due to the large amount of broken glass and slivers of wood at the top. The surface was a sandy one and we walked about in all directions to get the views. We took many photos to commemorate our climb and we began the descent to Carter Notch. This part I remembered. It is straight down on boulders. I was glad that I had not seen them the first time around or I never would have attempted it. We arrived at the lakes and stopped for a lunch. We sat on the rocks along the shore watching the minnows in the water beside us. It was very relaxing. Mike and I went into the hut to look for the book I had signed on my birthday trip with Mary Gaudreau, but we could not find the register. I was disappointed. Everything looked so normal in the bright daylight that it seemed like a totally different place. I missed having my imagination run wild in the fog and darkness. It did not make sense to linger since the Seaveys were waiting for us at the cars, so we left along the Nineteen Mile Brook Trail to get back to the highway.

I could not believe how long the trail out was. It was a wonder that Mary and I ever made it in! We went on and on forever. We formed two groups again with Carol Pearson and I bringing up the rear from a long distance behind. We passed the time telling jokes and getting to know each other. We found that we had quite a bit in common and planned to do a few more hikes this year. At one point we passed a lady leading a group of women up Carter Dome. She had done the four thousand footers a few years ago and was repeating most of them with her friends and her daughter. Her sense of humor was catching and Carol and I left her smiling. We soon found ourselves on the final leg of our journey heralded by the sound of cars zooming along on the highway… a most welcome sound. We found Nancy and Carl drinking sodas at the car and studying for their college exams. They had used the time wisely!

We took a wonderfully cooling dip in Lake Chocorua on the way home. Mike had spotted snakes swimming further down the beach by the bridge but decided not to tell me about it until after my swim for which I was grateful. I guess he did not want to see me running on the water after such a nice hike.

Hey, Lady!

THE TRIPYRAMIDS

NORTH TRIPYRAMID
Elevation: 4140
MIDDLE TRIPYRAMID
Elevation: 4110
Date: **August 17, 1992**
Trails: **Pine Bend Brook Trail**
Sabbaday Brook Trail

CARLA MARVIN was interested in doing a climb on her summer vacation time and my surgical unit was not busy. Art Batchelder, my friend Joan's husband, was interested in starting on his forty-eight mountains, had not done the Tripyramids, and was interested in joining us. He would do the hike with us and go on to camp out in the woods and head over to Mount Whiteface in the morning by himself.

Since he was up there hiking other trails already, we agreed to pick up Art on the Kancamagus Highway. Carla and I met early and had a light breakfast on the highway on the ride up Route 16. The day dawned - a perfect summer day. High clouds and a dry warmth in the air with just a hint of a breeze to shoo the bugs away. I must admit that I was a bit uncomfortable about hiking with Art because he had recently finished the Appalachian Trail from Georgia to Maine. I figured he would leave me behind in a cloud of dust, or worse, he would hang back watching me hike. We did manage to stack the deck in our favor since Carla and I were able to light pack, while Art had all the gear necessary for a few days out in the wilderness. In retrospect, that fact sort of balanced things out.

We found Art at the appointed spot, and he followed us the half mile or so to the selected trailhead parking area. In a very short time, we arranged our packs and started off on the trail. The hike up was relatively easy with a gentle grade to it. We had Art lead, and he had no problem following the trail. Carla and I were not so lucky. Art pointed out the signs several times, but we could not seem to tell the real signs from the ones that Nature makes on its own. The blazes seemed to consist of twenty year old hatchet marks on birch trees. To me, the blazes resembled the scars that form naturally on these tender trees. We complacently followed Art along. The birds on this hike were particularly noteworthy and we listened to the songs of at least twenty or so different birds. We tried to identify them with the aid of binoculars, but we were unable to pinpoint many of them. We did manage to startle a grouse whose noisy flight to safety took our collective breath away. They are very noisy birds. We were able to take the frequent breaks I need, and talked companionably as we rested, ate gorp, and drank water. At one point, we shared Carla's new climbing idea, a bagel and cream cheese. That was mighty tasty with the Tang that I had mixed in my extra water bottle. As we approached the top, the way became steeper. I remember Art giving me a bit of a boost from behind when I was trying to heave myself up over a particularly steep part of the trail. I returned the favor by pulling him up behind me. Carla was able to do it on her own and laughed at our team antics! In retrospect, we probably made quite a spectacle from behind. By that point, I was wondering if we would ever attain the summit. We seemed to have been walking forever, and though we could see how much we had progressed by turning around and viewing the trail and the scenery below, we had no signs to encourage us. I felt like we might have to walk forever. I was also nervous that while we were fooling around, we may have missed a trail sign. Art and Carla seemed to be doing all right, so I tried to shake off the uncomfortable feelings and enjoy the day. We were not talking much by then, choosing to put all our energy into climbing. I was finally able to get into the phase-out mode necessary to climb. At last we reached the top of North Tripyramid. The summit of this mountain sort of jumps out of the woods at you. You are hiking, and then you are at the top. We had added almost three quarters of an hour to the estimated guidebook time, but we had made it. We took a little time to crow over our success and took a few mug shots and funny photographs at the top. We were in high spirits. I had really come to enjoy Art's company and with Carla added for balance, we were a good group.

We passed the sign for the Sabbaday Brook Trail shortly after we left the first summit and hiked on to Middle Tripyramid. This peak was somewhat obscured by high brush, but it was easy to get to several outlooks to enjoy the scenery and take pictures. We enjoyed a leisurely lunch together with Art amusing us with stories of his infamous hike. He had many tales about the people he had walked some of the miles with, including a blind man with his specially trained dog. The stories were fantastic and if I could have left that peak and started for Georgia at that moment, I would have. He made it sound so wonderful!

After a good rest and more photo taking, we began to repack our gear. We gave Art the balance of our food for the next leg of his journey and bid him a fond farewell as he charted his next steps on the map. Carla and I decided to take the Sabbaday Brook Trail down to the highway. It would save backtracking all the way and we would come out less than a mile from the car. It seemed like a good idea at the time. We figured out that we had to go down the slide and we did so with great gusto and much laughter. At one point, I saw many footprints and we got off the slide to follow them. We were pretty sure that it was the trail. I hoped that whoever made these prints knew where they were going, because we did not. We decided to trust the footprints and we tracked them most of the way out. Finally, about a quarter of a mile from the highway, there appeared a single arrow. We were out. We did not go see the spectacular falls because the sky was threatening. Instead we found our way to the highway and walked back to the car. The rain started the same moment I put my key in the ignition. Someone was watching out for us that day, that's for sure!

Hey, Lady!

MOUNT MORIAH

Elevation: 4049
Date: August 30, 1992
Trails: Stoney Brook Trail
           Carter Moriah Trail

CAROL PEARSON and I had not seen much of each other since the hike to the Carters earlier in the month. She had been climbing with Nancy Seavey, and our times off never seemed to coordinate. Finally a time period arrived in which we had days off together and we made arrangements to go out. We agreed to climb Mount Moriah in the latter part of August. Art, my friend from the Tripyramids, wanted to climb Moriah. We had our little group set and planned to meet in the parking area by seven o'clock in the morning. Carol and I were primed to have a good day. We talked and laughed most of the way up the highway. Carol's father has given her a lifetime supply of New England humor-type jokes with double meanings and many railroad humor jokes. We arrived at the parking area and found Art already there, asleep in his car. He had made a commitment to drive a man to Maine and begged off accompanying us on the hike. He stayed while we donned our boots and was horrified by my stained lucky sock liners that I had been wearing for most of my hikes. I was slightly embarrassed as I refused his offer of sparkling white new sock liners but he understood immediately when I explained the history of my own liners.

The trailhead was very easy to find and Carol and I set out to conquer the peak. There was some confusion between the two reference books on climbing for the area. Carol's book stated that this climb would take about six and a half hours, while the *AMC Guidebook* said it would take eight hours. We did the round trip in about seven hours walking time-eliminating the time we took for breaks and lunch. The trail was laid out well along the lay of the land. The area around this path is gorgeous with many spots to rest one's feet in gently-flowing brooks and on sun-warmed stones. Carol and I were able to keep a conversation flowing for most of the first part of the trail without getting too breathless. Carol readily accepted my mandatory two minute breaks every half hour and five minute breaks every hour. Doing a hike in this manner keeps me going and actually helps me stay on guidebook time.

I began to have a problem with my left foot by the time we reached the Carter Moriah Trail. It hurt to put weight on the inner part of my arch. This does not make for easy walking, and I found going on a bit difficult. Carol had an extra set of foam inserts and I used them without significant relief. The problem lasted about two hours. This was a new problem and I hoped it was not related to my leg pain. The pain in my leg did not change significantly with this new development so we pushed onwards with a bit more attention being paid to my lower extremity. The hike along the ridge was absolutely beautiful and made up for the lengthy part through the woods which had seemed to drag. The peak itself seemed difficult to find. Nancy had done this climb and had described the top, and though we stopped at three separate areas thinking that surely this was the goal, we could not see the bench mark Nancy had mentioned. We even broke for lunch at one point to celebrate our completion, only to meet a group of hikers from Vermont College, who showed us that we had a way to go. It was a bit disheartening, but since the rest of the way involved going along the ridge, and culminated in a steep rock climb like the chimney that I had enjoyed on Mount Osceola, it did not matter. We took a second lunch break beside the elusive bench mark. We lay back after the meal and watched the birds in the area. We saw a huge raven who shouted his disapproval at our presence and a high-soaring bird that one of the college students recognized as an eagle by its flight pattern. We enjoyed sharing the top with these informative young people. Being tuned in by these folks, we were able to see many birds on the way out that we might have missed otherwise, including a grouse whose sudden departure nearly scared me to death! It was hard for us to leave the ridge with beautiful scenery to reenter the wooded part of the trail. I hated to leave the scenery. Carol hated to leave the blueberries we had overlooked on the way in.

We kept up a good pace all the way down the trail and I was finally able to indulge myself in another long-lived fantasy I had harbored since starting to climb. I have been simply entranced by the various pools of water that the brooks have cut

Hey, Lady!

into the rocks. I may have mentioned that I have this thing for freezing myself in ponds, and this seemed to be a logical extension for this little quirk. We arrived at a foot bridge and there were no signs posted to prohibit swimming. In fact, it was obvious that this area was used quite often as a camping spot, though it surely did not qualify under the standards for camping set by the books. Carol and I left the trail and went down by the water to check it out. I did not see any obvious dangers or alien creatures in the water. It seemed cold and inviting. Carol agreed to go back on the footbridge to warn me if any other hikers were to approach the area. With much trepidation, I disrobed. In retrospect, I am not quite sure what my plan was if anyone had come along. Perhaps I thought I could hide my 160+ pound frame behind the two five inch trees and the three foot high rock upon which I had so carefully laid my clothes. Fortunately I was not put to the test. The water fulfilled all my expectations and I enjoyed paddling around for quite some time. Carol seemed content to sit on the bridge. She kept watch and occasionally made questionable remarks. I was having a great time. The pool was quite deep and the rocks on the bottom were eroded to smooth perfection. By the bridge, the water picked up speed and I could feel the current rush by. I looked up to see my new pal snap a picture—great! I beat a hasty retreat and joined Carol on the bridge, offering her many different bribes for the film. She was not interested in any of them. The rest of the hike was uneventful and we soon found ourselves out of the woods and on the highway. We set a course for the Pizza Barn off Route 16 and celebrated our success! After showing the Seaveys, Carol presented me with the photograph, but not the negative.

MOUNT CARRIGAIN

Elevation: 4680
Date: September 12, 1992
Trail: Signal Ridge Trail

SINCE THE hike up Moriah, I had been living in a state of tension. I was sure that something would prevent me from achieving my goal of joining the Four Thousand Footer Club. It was hard to be within one hike of accomplishing that task. I was concerned about the increasing leg pain that I was experiencing, but I did not tell Mike or the doctors about it lest they reiterate the stupidity of my hiking. Jim Wilton, Carla, and the Seaveys told me that they could not join me this month, but if I waited until October, they would be sure to come along to

Hey, Lady!

help me celebrate. It was too stressful not to go as soon as possible. I was afraid that if I waited, I would not have the strength to make the climb. Gaylene Chaloult from the X-ray department and Carol Pearson were the only ones available to go. The whole week before we left, I watched every step I took. I am prone to sprains and I was afraid I would sprain something and not be able to go. I could not have stood that!

We met at the hospital parking lot early in the morning and headed to Jeanine's for breakfast. Everything tasted like ashes to me because my stomach was tied in knots. I chose to drive to the trailhead to keep my mind occupied. For a bad start, I ran over a chipmunk on West Road. I prayed that it did not portend a bad adventure! We managed to arrive safely at the trailhead near the Sawyer River Road. We stretched the kinks out of our bodies and affixed our packs. I had never felt so jittery. I was a basket case! Mike sensed what I was thinking and came over to reassure me that things would be fine. We started up the Signal Ridge Trail.

The trail up to the summit is laid out very well giving maximum views. We were able to cross all the streams easily and I began to relax and enjoy the heat of the fall sun on my back and to breathe in the smell of the dirt and the trees along the trail. It has always amazed me that I am not aware of such odors in city parks, but become aware of them very quickly when I get into the forest. Maybe it is a question of being in tune with Nature. We met a great many people on this hike including a nurse from our local operating room and a man named McKinney who leads hikes for the AMC. He was taking his son up to the top for the day. There was also a forest ranger with his son. Walking was a bit more difficult for me on that climb. I was being careful not to fall or twist anything, but there was also an undercurrent of weakness that I had been aware of growing worse over the last few weeks. We all plodded along the trail... people coming up on us, passing us, coming down, all friendly and all smiling encouragement to me when they heard it was my last hike on the four thousand footer list. What a boost it was to see those smiles. I would take a deep breath and hustle forward. It was necessary to take many breaks, and the others adjusted their style to mine without complaint. We would make it together.

After four and a half hours we arrived at the old fire warden's cabin. We spent some time there to recover our breath and pop trail snacks into our mouths. We also discovered an old well that we explored before putting our packs back on for the final ascent. Mike took the pack from my back and hurried on ahead with the others to await my arrival, alone, at the top. I walked on, enjoying what would probably be my final hike, thinking private thoughts. I was rudely interrupted by the voices of my hike mates yelling at me to hurry up. I ran up the last hundred feet or so and burst onto the summit like Sylvester Stallone in Rocky. Cameras flashed around me as all my companions took photos to commemorate the occasion. Mike and I climbed up to the top of the observation tower and popped a bottle of ice cold champagne. We shared with all of those at the top. Poor Mr. McKinney had probably been awaiting my arrival for hours, considering how fast he had been hiking, but he had waited to congratulate me. That meant a lot to me! We put on extra clothes at the top and had a wonderful champagne lunch. For the first time, and probably the last, I enjoyed the taste of champagne! I had made it. I rested my head on a warm granite stone and felt the world turn around me as I looked up into a clear blue sky. Life was good.

Gaylene turned to me as we were packing up to begin our descent and reminded me that I would have to get back down

to have it count. I appreciated her sense of humor. It put things back into perspective. We all began the climb downwards. One of the best and most noticeable parts of this hike is the stand of birches along the top third of the hike. They are along the outer edge of the trail and they give the illusion of a curved staircase going up to the heavens. I took a shot of Carol standing ahead of us on the trail with the trees as a background. Since we were making such good time on the way out, I was again able to take a dip in one of the streams and was completely refreshed by the cold water and the warm rocks. No pictures this time! Again the Barbecue Pit was blessed by our company on the return ride home and Mike and I arrived in plenty of time to get ready for a square dance that evening. I had officially ended my forty-eighth four-thousand foot mountain and was qualified for membership in the Four-Thousand Footer Club!

Hey, Lady!

I SHOULD subtitle this section: "What I think I have finally figured out!" The following information is based on my own experiences combined with insights provided by my hiking companions. We have all shared common experiences, but we usually perceive things a bit differently. The information shared in this last chapter is what I have learned about hiking, equipment, and finally, myself.

AMC GUIDEBOOK: My hiking Bible. Frankly I would not take a step off the highway without this book in my hand. I do not agree with all of the trail descriptions and estimated times, but in my opinion it is the most accurate informational resource available for the White Mountains. The book includes maps of the region and trail descriptions. It is jam-packed with all the rules and regulations for hiking, camping, shuttles to and from hiking areas, clubs to join, information about animals and plants of the area, and important safety tips. All this is laid out in a simple format with references and indexes. It is compact enough to carry on a hike and is not expensive. The book may be found in most specialty shops for climbing as well as in some book stores.

BOOTS: I have come to realize that everyone's feet are different and what is wonderful for one person will cause agony to another. If there is one generality that will be true for all boots, it is that they need to have good support and a good sole. There is nothing more uncomfortable after a long day's hike than to wobble down over rocks worrying about spraining your ankles! It may seem unbelievable that tiny pebbles can feel like boulders if the sole of the boot does not absorb impact, but it is painfully true. These traits almost automatically eliminate wearing sneakers on the trail. Plan on trying on several brands of boots, seek the advice of knowledgeable salespeople, and read the information available in the stores before picking your boots. Plan on buying a few pairs before you are truly satisfied. Remember that the most expensive boot is not necessarily the best boot. If you find your ideal boot, be sure to buy a couple of pairs before the manufacturer decides to mess it up for you by making a new and improved model and eliminating yours from stock. Buy your socks and liners at the same time and in

Hey, Lady!

adequate amounts for the same reason. If you find a great combination for your feet... hoard your supply!

BUG REPELLENT: Try the oil. Try the sprays and the squirts and the roll-ons. Try the sheets and the screens. Try them all and good luck!

CAMPING: Always try all your equipment out before each trip. Follow the instructions regarding the care of the products you use. Practice setting up the tents in the backyard to see how much space you will actually need to get the tent up and to see for sure how many people the tent will accommodate. I have never seen a three person tent that could actually hold three adults. When the rain and wind is whipping around you is not the time to discover that it was really necessary to water proof the tent, that not enough stakes and tie-downs came with the kit, your flashlight batteries died, or that you needed a different kind of fuel for the new stove. I know all these things from personal experience. Remember to obey all the signs and the rules regarding tenting as presented on the signposts and as listed in the *Guidebook.*

CLOTHING: It will be necessary to find your own personal style of clothes for hiking. Start with comfortable clothes you already own and be open to new things. I would not spend much money until you know for sure what will work for you. Personally I went from stretch shorts with cotton tops to wide-legged nylon men's shorts and tee shirts. I added wool, which was a challenge for me to accept, and Gortex in gradual stages to where, after twenty or so years of hiking, I think I have it right for me... at least for now.

COMPANIONS: Be courteous and honest. Do not claim to be a slow-or a fast-hiker if you are not. It is very annoying to believe someone who says that they are so slow that they are worried about keeping up with you, and then find yourself left behind in a cloud of dust at the first trail marker. Constantly rushing to keep up makes your companion feel inadequate and rushed, to say nothing about missing all the scenery and fun a hike should consist of. It is just as bad thinking that your companion will keep up a good pace and having to turn back halfway up a mountain because it has taken two hours to hike a mile. You can turn a person completely off hiking by not being honest from the beginning. If you want to introduce a potential hiker to the sport, pick an easy trail and let them take the lead to set a pace that is comfortable for them. Hopefully with a few hikes, they will be able to move faster, if not, make a decision of whether or not their company makes up for having to go at a slower pace than what you normally like. If you can, check for AMC or other group sponsored hikes. They list the level of difficulty and will tell you what age groups are going to participate. It is a good way to find companions from different areas and of various levels of skill and speed for later independent hikes.

FIRST AID: I would advise everyone to take a first aid course. The AMC offers excellent courses, as do the Red Cross and the Scouting movements. Choose a course that leans heavily towards the outdoors, rather than industrial emergency. I have had multiple occasions to use my skills on myself, companions, and even strangers on the trail. It is a worthwhile investment. Be sure to carry a good first aid kit with each group and to have all pertinent medical information on all the group members along with you. Carry prescription drugs that you may require.

FOOD: Climbing burns calories, but I have not lost an ounce yet! In order to keep your energy level high enough to propel your body onward and upward, it is necessary to consume food. Bring foods that are easy to carry, do not crush or spoil easily, and that you like. It is also necessary to pack high energy snacks like fruit or candy. Always pack extras for yourself or for others in case of emergency.

MAPS/COMPASS: I would strongly advise that you take a course in map and compass reading and sincerely hope that you do better at it than I do. I have taken courses with a navigator, my hunter husband, the Girl Scouts, and the AMC, and I still cannot always relate to the concepts. I do see the need to understand and will keep trying! I think I got turned around in second grade when I somehow misunderstood the concept that North is North, not whatever direction that I was facing. I do the same thing with road maps... I tend to think that no matter what direction I am going in, it is always toward the upper part of the map. Obviously I still need a little work in this area.

PACKS: You will probably buy three or four packs before you find the perfect one for yourself. Therefore, I would strongly advise borrowing from friends or renting from the sporting stores before investing a lot of money. There are so many major decisions about types and styles that it is not possible to make a definite decision without actually taking a hike with it on and carrying actual weight on your shoulders. Most packs are very comfortable and light when they are empty! Incidentally, the same goes for stoves, tents, and other major equipment… always share, borrow or rent. Try before you buy!

PERSONAL HYGIENE: Do not pollute the streams or the trails with your waste. Use courtesy and common sense. Follow the instructions found in any trail book about proper etiquette. Carry your paper in and carry it out. Do not use facial tissue because it is not biodegradable. Use biodegradable toilet paper… please!

PHYSICAL CONDITION: I firmly believe that the forests, waterfalls, and the mountains are here for everyone to enjoy. That is part of my reason for writing this book. I do not think it would be wise to get up off the couch and set out to conquer Mount Washington. Clear it with your doctor if you have led a sedentary lifestyle for a while. Build up to it. Take a few walks around your town. Take short walks that build up to longer ones. Go see a waterfall in the woods. Build up your endurance. Then pick a short trail with a good reward. Set easy goals for yourself at first and build up to the biggies. I would hazard a guess that if you can do about five miles on level to hilly terrain around your hometown in a couple of hours without experiencing difficulty, you can probably do one of the four thousand footers.

STORES: If a salesperson does not ask you how often you are planning on hiking, where you will be going, and what your experience is… leave the store! He cannot sell you the proper gear without this rudimentary knowledge even if he resembles Sir Edmund Hillary himself. As the consumer, it is your re-

Hey, Lady!

sponsibility to find someone to help you. Be wise and know that the most expensive is not always the best.

SWIMMING: Please watch for posted areas and be aware that some streams are the local water supply. The streams are almost always bitterly cold and are often dangerous due to the slippery rocks, and surprisingly strong water flow. If, like me, you cannot resist a quick dip, be careful.

TRAIL MARKERS: Cairns are piles of rocks and the idea is to go from pile to pile. These trail markers are great when the weather is bad and visibility is poor. You stand a good chance of tripping over one if you do not actually see it first. Blazes are splashes of paint on trees and rocks or cuts in the trees. Each trail has a blaze at the beginning and the idea is to go from blaze to blaze. They are sometimes color-coded by club and trail. You will soon notice that when you think you may be lost, even if you are not, you will never see a blaze without hunting up and down the trail. However, when you are on a straight trail without any turnoffs or stream crossings, there are always a multitude of blazes about. Posted trail signs are rare and treasured. They not only assure you that you are in the right state, they even tell you how far you have to go to get to where you want to be.

WATER: Water is essential and hard to find in some areas in the White Mountains. Water is also heavy! If you know for sure that you will have a supply of water available to you, perhaps one canteen per person, along with a water filtration device would be sufficient. If you are unsure, plan on taking more than one canteen per person. I have a nice method that works wonderfully for me. I fill my canteen half full the night before I go on a hike and put it in the freezer. I top off the ice in the morning with additional water. I bought Mike a wonderful two quart canteen and always mention how happy I am to see him use this gift. I lovingly offer to fill his canteen to the brim with the coldest water I can get. On the trail, I share his water and hoard mine. By afternoon, most of my ice is melted, but the water remains very cold and refreshing. All in all, I am pleased with this system!

Finally, what have I learned about myself? I know that beneath this exterior shell I call my body is a hiker! I have learned how to set a goal and how to reach it. I have found that I have inner strengths and resources available to me because I have tapped them. I know that no matter what life throws my way, I will be able to cope with it. Hiking has given me an inner sense of peace, confidence, and a security that cannot be found outside of one's self. I have a sense of responsibility—almost a stewardship—towards Nature. This is no burden to bear, but an honor. It gives a sense of purpose and permanence to my life. I have climbed against some pretty bad odds to achieve the goal I set for myself, but I endured... succeeded... and because of this, I will never be the same. I will forever enjoy hiking in the mountains.

Hey, Lady!

JUDY'S GLOSSARY

FRIENDS SUGGESTED that some of the vocabulary would not be understood by everyone and therefore I should include a brief glossary.

AMC—APPALACHIAN MOUNTAIN CLUB: A group organized in 1876 which makes it the oldest mountain club in the
USA They are based in Boston, Massachusetts, and have nu-
merous publications and year-round lecture series to benefit
the enjoyment of the mountains. The AMC has several huts
spread throughout the mountains. For a fee you may stay at
the hut for the night which cuts down on the things you have
to carry for survival. The huts usually include a full home-
cooked supper, a place to sleep with pillow and blankets, breakfast, and often entertainment!

BLACK TOES: What you get when your boots are a hair too
tight and you walk downhill at a good clip. Doctors are
oftentimes horrified at the sight of black toenails.

BUSHWHACK: Using a compass and no blazes or signs to get
to a set point.

CAT SCRATCHES: Small trenches dug to bury human waste.
Ideally these are about six inches deep.

CREW: A crew member, singular or plural, is a person who
mans, or womans the huts of the AMC Hut System. These
young people prepare the meals, tend the huts, run experiments
of various kinds, and are trained in Mountain Rescue and First
Aid.

FOUR-THOUSAND FOOTER CLUB OF NEW HAMPSHIRE
A group formed in 1957. To qualify for membership, one must
climb to and from the summits of each of the forty-eight mountains on the list.

GORP: Trail mix made of basically peanuts, raisins, and M&M's.

GRADE: There is a balance between the horizontal gain and the vertical rise. I cannot get this straight, but I do know that the greater the vertical rise, the more strenuous the hike is. The closer the little lines are together on the topographical maps, the greater the vertical rise. So, if the little lines are on top of each other, or the book gives a great vertical rise number, brace yourself for a steep hike!

LEAN-TO: Shelter to rest or to camp in.

OUTCROPS: Large rocks projecting out of the earth. Some are positioned for great viewing.

RAVINE: Steep-sided valley

RESTRICTED USE AREAS: Controlled areas where no camping, fires, or stoves are allowed. For more information see the AMC Guide or the White Mountain National Forest.

SWITCHBACKS: When a trail is too steep for safe climbing, or the risk of erosion is too great, a switchback is used to ease the problem. A switchback cuts across the side of a mountain and creates an easier grade. There are usually a couple of switchbacks that go up and back and forth across the area. Switchbacks may seem to add mileage to a climb, but they make it easier.

TRAIL: A marked path to follow to a specified destination.

TRAILHEAD: The starting point of a trail.

TRAIL SIGNS: Wooden signs with mileage to various destinations carved into them.

TREELINE: The last point to relieve yourself with any privacy. Trees do not grow above the treeline. Not to be confused with timberline which is where the commercially used lumber line is reached.

THE 4000 FOOTERS OF NEW HAMPSHIRE

Hey, Lady!